This book belongs to:

_____

_____

Date

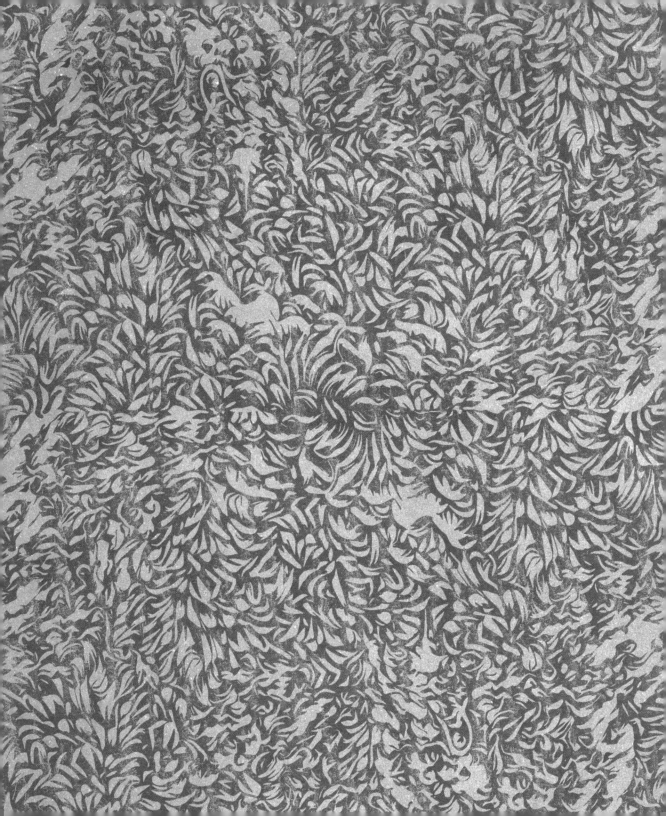

NOTE-TAKING EDITION

HONEST PRAYERS

FOR

Mama Bears

HILLARY MORGAN FERRER

with **JULIE LOOS**

HARVEST HOUSE PUBLISHERS
EUGENE, OREGON

Unless otherwise indicated, all Scripture are taken from the Holy Bible, New International Version®, NIV®. Copyright © 1973, 1978, 1984, 2011 by Biblica, Inc.™ Used by permission of Zondervan. All rights reserved worldwide. www.zonder -van.com. The "NIV" and "New International Version" are trademarks registered in the United States Patent and Trademark Office by Biblica, Inc.™

Verses marked NASB are taken from the (NASB®) New American Standard Bible®, Copyright © 1960, 1971, 1977, 1995, 2020 by The Lockman Foundation. Used by permission. All rights reserved. www.lockman.org

Verses marked NET are quoted from the NET Bible®, https://netbible.com. Copyright © 1996, 2019. Used by permission from Biblical Studies Press, LLC. All rights reserved.

Cover design by Faceout Studio, Molly von Borstel

Cover images © Denis Sarbashev, U-Design, Phatthanit, Inhabitant B / Shutterstock; esa / Adobe Stock

Interior design by Chad Dougherty

For bulk, special sales, or ministry purchases, please call 1-800-547-8979. Email: Customerservice@hhpbooks.com

This logo is a federally registered trademark of the Hawkins Children's LLC. Harvest House Publishers, Inc., is the exclusive licensee of this trademark.

Honest Prayers for Mama Bears Note-Taking Edition

Copyright © 2024 by Hillary Morgan Ferrer
Published by Harvest House Publishers
Eugene, Oregon 97408
www.harvesthousepublishers.com

ISBN 978-0-7369-9010-3 (Hardcover)

Printed in China

24 25 26 27 28 29 30 31 32 / RDS / 10 9 8 7 6 5 4 3 2 1

Hillary:

This book is for all the Mama Bears who have bought into
the lie that their prayers need to be eloquent. They don't.
My desire is that this book sets you free from the self-condemning
voice that discourages you from coming to God because you
think you're "not good at prayer." Nah. Just say it all, Mama Bears,
and then turn toward the truth of His Word.
Everyone has to start somewhere.

Julie:

To my paternal grandmother, Henrietta "Tom" Dalton,
who modeled what it meant to be a praying woman and prayed
for me more than I will ever know. To my first grandchild,
Anna Ruth Loos, and my future grandchildren, whom I
promise to pray for, and to my daughters-in-law Mary and Sarah
as they become praying Mama Bears. To my Lord and Savior,
Jesus Christ, who intercedes for me.

Contents

Section 1: Selfless Prayers for Self

Section 2: Spiritual Protection for the Home Turf

Section 3: From Bzzzz!!! to Zzzzz...: Short Prayers for the Daily Grind

Section 4: From My Bean to My Bean's Bean: Ages, Stages, and Rhythms of Life

Section 5: From Clay to Vessel: Prayers for My Kids' Spiritual Formation

Section 6: Things My Kids Have to Deal With

Section 7: Welcome to the Rumblllllle

Section 8: Does This Prayer Make Me Look Fat?

Section 9: When. I. Just. Can't. Even.

Section 12: Church, State, School, and Culture

Contributors

Julie and I would like to acknowledge the Mama Bears who contributed prayers (or ideas for prayers):

Blankenship, Kristi

Bowen, Andrea

Burchfield, Halee

Cannon, Teasi

Collins, Mary

Cox, Robin

Cramer, Alexa

Cummings, Sarah

Davison, Amy

DeFrates, Jennifer

Dyson, Elizabeth

(Ferrer, Hillary)

Francis, Amanda

Hox, Kate

Huxley, Kim

Johnson, Karen

Jones, Allison

Joseph, Heather

Kennedy, Katie

Lenz, Shannon

Long, Erin

(Loos, Julie)

Patrick, Karen

Seago, Koren

Short, Hillary

Slomkowski, Mary

(Spirit, Holy ☺)

Talsma, Tanya

Troja, Cassie

Wolcott, David

Wotring, Meghan

An Honest Introduction

Hillary Morgan Ferrer

I grew up in the church and was always interested in the things of God. I knew I was supposed to pray, but I wasn't quite sure how. To this day, I have notebooks full of prayer lists that I made in junior high and high school. (I wrote my prayers out because my mind would wander if I tried to pray silently.) There is nothing profound in those prayers. I'm embarrassed to admit that I mostly prayed for popularity and for boys to like me. (Give me a break! I was in junior high. That's what junior high girls think about!) Even in those meager attempts to follow God, the Lord developed in me the habit of coming to Him with my uncensored thoughts—praying what was actually on my mind, not what I thought *should* be on my mind. The shamelessness of those prayers cultivated an honesty in talking to God. And that honesty led me to pray a prayer that essentially changed my life.

I was in the ninth grade, and our Bible study leader started a New Year's tradition where we wrote letters to ourselves documenting the past year and making projections for the future. We had places to list our closest friends, what the best and worst parts of the year had been, and where we saw ourselves in one year, five years, and ten years. Then, at the end, we wrote out a prayer. The prayer I wrote in December 1993 became the model for my prayer life from that point forward:

Lord, I don't really want You…but I want to want You.

Talk about honest! Who straight-up tells God that she has no interest in Him, but that she kinda wants to? Me, that's who. By this time, I knew what prayers "should" sound like, but I had practiced being honest with the Lord for so many years that when I matured enough to pray for something that really mattered, I didn't feel pressured to sugarcoat it. The Lord knew my heart. He knew if I desired Him or not. Why pretend to be anything other than what I was? It's not like I had lost my interest in following God. I wasn't in any kind of rebellion. However, I heard people talking about having a desire and yearning for the Lord, and I knew that—emotionally—I didn't have that. But I really wanted to! Starting that ninth-grade year, I saw the Lord faithfully answer that prayer, slowly changing me from a "good Christian girl" into an avid disciple.

That one simple prayer served as the "aha moment" for the rest of my life. And an aha moment is my hope for you and the prayers in this book. Often, we are so consumed with what we think our prayers *should* sound like that we neglect to say what we are actually thinking. God knows our thoughts! He's not going to be surprised that we're not more "spiritual sounding." There's nothing in Scripture about Him valuing elegant prayers more than simple ones. (Just the opposite, really.) So why not come to Him *as we are* since He already knows? Picture your kids coming to you like, "Oh, thou art my wholesome parental unit! Wilt thou doth grant me this sugary confection that delighteth my eyes and bringeth joy to mine heart?" rather than "I want a cookie." If it's right before dinner, the answer is no either way. And if we're at a carnival, it's probably yes either way!

HONEST VERSUS SHALLOW

Now, there is a difference between shallow prayers and honest prayers. Shallow prayers are honest, but they aren't always effective (like my old junior high prayers). I'd liken a shallow prayer to a list of things we just want, as if we are a child making our Christmas wish list for Santa Claus. There's nothing wrong with asking for the things we want, but those aren't always the most effective prayers—because, as James 4:3 says, "When you ask, you do not receive, because you ask with wrong motives, that you may spend what you get on your pleasures."

An honest prayer is one in which you are willing to sound stupid, say the wrong thing, or admit things out loud that might be embar-rassing for someone to hear. When we try and dress up our prayers, we aren't fooling God. More often than not, we are fooling ourselves.

THE GOALS OF THIS BOOK

Julie and I have a few different goals for this book. One goal is for these prayers to give you *permission* to say things to God that you haven't said before. Many prayers were intentionally crafted to express the raw emotion that can accompany motherhood.

But raw emotion alone is not always helpful. If we end there, we haven't done our job! Our other goal in crafting honest prayers is to model what it looks like to renew our minds (Romans 12:2), especially by focusing on gratitude. What I've discovered in my years of walking with the Lord is that something profound happens when I can get out all the yuck (the honest part), and then refocus my thoughts on bib-lical truth (the renewing part). It's a great recipe for a heart that God can mold.

Our third goal was to make this book a truly communal experience. While Julie and I wrote many of the prayers, we have contributions from Mama Bears from all walks of life and stages of motherhood. We have prayers in here from official Mama Bears, Mama Bears who were on our launch team, and even friends and family who made unique contributions. We have prayers from single Mama Bears, adoptive Mama Bears, blended-family Mama Bears, and Grandmama Bears. I wanted the prayers to be anonymous so each person would have the freedom to be personal and specific without having to worry who would read the prayer. And though Julie and I edited the prayers to have a cohesive tone, the voices behind them are many. Because we are better together!

Finally, while I love that people are reading this book and praying through these prayers, I have a more profound goal: that, one day, you will not need this book anymore! As you read these prayers, my hope is that you will learn how to craft honest prayers for yourself, learning how to speak authentically about where you are and then intentionally about how you'd like to see God move—specifically and according to His will and character. It's okay if you're not some prayer guru! Everyone struggles with prayer. It's when we give ourselves permission to struggle—and even to fail—that we also find the strength to get back up and try again.

AN INTRODUCTION TO THE SECTIONS

Section 1 is near and dear to my heart because it addresses the misconception that it is selfish to pray for ourselves. When women pray, it's often for other people. We pray for our husbands, for our children, for our friends and family. But what about praying for ourselves? Does this make you feel a little uncomfortable? If so, you're not alone, and your reasons are most likely very noble. But I would like to make the argument that praying for ourselves is one of the *most important things we can do as Mama Bears.*

I suspect we believe that praying for ourselves is selfish because we don't know what we should be praying for. When we pray for others, our words often revolve around comfort, peace, success, and health. It feels right to pray this way for others, but asking for our own comfort and prosperity? Well, that just feels a bit gross.

Truth is, these aren't necessarily bad things to ask God for. He is a good Father who delights in giving good gifts to His children (Matthew 7:11). But I wonder if praying for ourselves might become more natural if we looked a little further upstream, so to speak. Rather than asking for outcomes (such as health, prosperity, and comfort), what if we prayed for righteous *desires*? It's the "give a man a fish and he eats for a day; teach a man to fish and he eats for a lifetime" principle. Pray for the desired outcome, and you may get it once. Ask the Lord to change your desires, cravings, habits, and heart, and you will affect a thousand outcomes in the future. (Now, praying this prayer doesn't give us permission *not* to act if we don't "feel" like it. But man, isn't it easier to obey when you truly want to?)

When we begin to pray for the right *desires*, we're not just praying for outcomes; we're praying for faithfulness through the process. And when we grow in faithfulness, our character, patience, struggles, repentance, victories, and yes, even our failures, serve as valuable discipleship opportunities for our children. Walking the Christian life is hard! Sanctification (the process of ridding ourselves of sin and replacing it with obedience) is hard. It's a slow, steady process of disciplining our wills—and then allowing our hearts to follow. Praying to crave the Word, to desire the things of God, to cultivate healthy habits, and for the Lord to gently remove the chaff from our lives is the *opposite* of selfish. As with all the prayers in this book, it is our Mama Bear hope that you would use them as a launching point to find words specifically tailored to you and your own struggles.

Section 2 is centered around spiritual warfare as a necessary discipline. I realize the discussion on spiritual warfare can be complicated and even controversial in the church. There is some "in-house" debate on what spiritual warfare is and how we should pray warfare prayers without slipping into occult fascination. With all that in mind, we tend to agree with C.S. Lewis in the preface of *The Screwtape Letters*: "There are two equal and opposite errors into which our race can fall about the devils. One is to disbelieve in their existence. The other is to believe, and to feel an excessive and unhealthy interest in them. They themselves are equally pleased by both errors and hail a materialist or a magician with the same delight."

We Mama Bears have personally experienced these two unhealthy extremes in our Christian communities. Some people think a malevolent spirit is behind *everything* that must be discerned, named, and rebuked before anyone moves another inch. And then there's the "devil made me do it" crowd. Um…no. The devil didn't *make you* do anything. You done-did-it because your heart was like, "That sounds super satisfying! I'm totally in!" Friends, we don't need the devil to make us do anything. Our sinful desires are entirely sufficient (James 1:14).

That being said, neither should we ignore or forget that harmful spirits exist, and they love to sow seeds of jealousy, bitterness, lust, etc. They do it very, very well. And they *luuuurve* when we are completely oblivious to their schemes.

So these prayers are for praying over the various rooms of your house or the other places where you or your family spend time. I recommend praying over your home spaces regularly. We don't need to over spiritualize, but neither should we ignore the authority we have to dedicate our homes to Christ.

Section 3 is meant to take the Mama Bear through her day. We encourage you to type these up and post them around your house, or (if you're feeling feisty) to memorize them! There is something comforting about quieting your soul with a quick liturgy as you go about your day, from the moment your alarm goes off (Bzzzz!) to the moment you finally drift off to sleep (Zzzz...).

In section 4, we zoom out a bit—focusing on the needs and concerns of various phases we Mama Bears might go through. Our parental role changes over time as we respond to each developmental stage of our children—from the moment we first see our little bean on the sonogram, to when our grown-up bean posts a sonogram of their own little bean! Each stage is its own kind of beautiful and its own kind of hard—and both will pass in God's timing (which, according to empty nesters, is in the blink of an eye).

Sections 5 and 6 are dedicated to our cubs—the regular prayers that everyone needs for spiritual formation and the specific prayers our kids need for the world in which they are growing up.

Sections 7 through 10 are focused more on things Mama Bears have to deal with, from interpersonal conflicts (section seven) to the exhaustion of motherhood in this crazy culture (chapter nine).

Sections 11 and 12 are self-explanatory.

A FEW MORE THINGS YOU'LL WANT TO KNOW...

We at Mama Bear Apologetics have always been about practicality, so we couldn't just leave you with prayers! Pay attention to the additional activities, ideas, encouragements, or journaling exercises that are included with some of the prayers.

Furthermore, we tried to create a template for you to personalize these prayers as much as possible. Anytime you see [brackets], take them as a cue to insert your own information. Mostly it is a cue for you to insert your child's specific name. Occasionally, we include instructions for things to add to the prayer that will make it more personal, almost like Mad Libs.

How you read the book is up to you. Find the prayer(s) you need for the day and read according to need. Or, read the book straight through—almost as a devotional or tutorial on how to begin praying honestly with God about the things you have faced or will face as a mom. When those subjects arise, you will know you can go back to this book for help in praying over that issue. Praying through the book can also grow your compassion for fellow moms who may be going through something you currently are not. Share the prayer with them or pray it on their behalf. Julie and I pray this book will bless you and deepen your relationship with the Lord, and that it is as much of a blessing for you to read as it was for us to write.

Raising Dragon Slayers in an Era of Dragons

Jennifer DeFrates

Dear Lord, I am not sure I'm prepared to parent children in today's world. Sometimes just keeping my kids alive feels like an insurmountable hurdle, and I don't always feel confident in my ability to guide, protect, and nurture them well in this political and religious climate. I remember it was hard enough to be a Christian when the predominant culture was Christian. Especially as a teenager and young adult, it's incredibly hard to avoid sin, even when surrounded by fellow believers who are encouraging and supportive. Right now, I am scared for my children growing up in a world that blatantly celebrates sinfulness in so many ways and bombards them from every direction with flawed and deceptive definitions of love, identity, and truth.

Lord, I need You to strengthen me as a parent and believer. Open my mind to solid theology and doctrine as I study Your Word each day. Grant me wisdom so I may raise my children to think biblically and rationally through every issue they will face. Give me the courage to gently speak truth when our world distorts what Your Word says about our bodies, minds, behaviors, and beliefs. Help me be an example of living my beliefs boldly, even though I may be condemned as a bigot or worse. Sometimes upholding biblical truth is terrifying in this post-Christian culture. Make me wise enough to know when to be silent and brave enough to know when to speak. And may it all be wrapped in Your love and kindness.

As a parent, show me how to raise my children to see the image of God in all people first and to treat them as immortal souls whom

God has designed and created for a purpose. Let the Holy Spirit work through me to demonstrate Your perfect grace and mercy in the way I treat everyone so that my children see what it looks like to love others well. Open doors for me to share the gospel often in front of my children. I don't want to be a Christian in name only.

Help us wisely choose the entertainment we enjoy as a family; may it be honoring and glorifying to You. Help me protect and nurture my children's hearts and minds while inoculating them against culture's lies.

Lastly, Lord, I beg You to work within my children. Create a strong faith in them. Help them to know You personally and have their own faith and convictions. I don't want them to just parrot my beliefs and never know You for themselves. Forgive me for the times I feel overwhelmed by fear and anxiety about the persecution my children might face if they stand firm in their convictions as believers. Give me peace knowing that You will carry them through anything if they lean into deep fellowship with You. Even things that can bring physical suffering or destruction are not to be feared when they trust in You.

Help me remember that You appointed them to be born in such a time as this, and that You have prepared good works for them to do (Ephesians 2:10). In an era of dragons, You are raising up dragon slayers. Thank You for the strengths I see in my children. May they be mighty warriors in and for Your kingdom. In Your name I pray, amen.

Section 1

SELFLESS PRAYERS FOR SELF

Craving for the Word

Lord Jesus, You *are* the Word of God. When I crave the Word, I crave You. I pray that You would give me an insatiable desire for the Word, and for it to stay in my memory. I pray that when I am seeking guidance, You would turn my heart toward reading Your eternal truths.

I pray that when I miss my quiet time, You would give me discomfort, like when I'm hungry or thirsty. And when I feel like I can't retain information, please help me to remember Your words. When I sit and pray, when I love, when I discipline, or when I'm just going about my duties for the day, may Your words be ever present in my mind.

I pray for a godly pleasure as I study, that reading Your words would fill me with joy. Please bring others into my path who will study with me. I pray that You would highlight the resources that will help me understand Your Word better.

Oh God, Your Word is a lamp unto my feet and a light unto my path (Psalm 119:105). Help me to faithfully seek Your words even when reading feels like a chore. I trust You, Lord, to mold me into the image of Your only begotten Son. May every cell in my being crave the knowledge that comes from Your Word.

2

Eternal Perspective

God, I want to invest in what will last into eternity, but the petty things of the world keep taking my attention. I know this world is temporary and that all things here will eventually pass away, so please reform my perspective and help me prioritize what matters most. I pray that You would give me the spiritual eyes to see the things that will have eternal weight, no matter how mundane they may feel in the here and now. Lord, I know there are some battles that need to be fought, and other battles are just distractions. Please give me the wisdom to tell the difference. If there is anything I am fixating upon that's keeping me from eternal things, please reveal it to me.

You have put so many good things in my path, but they are not my ultimate things. Some good things may not be my responsibility. My primary tasks are being Your daughter, nurturing my marriage, and shepherding my children. Lord, may I be faithful to that which You have given me, knowing the fruits of my obedience will last after I am gone. I praise You that I have more than just this life to live for. Help me to live it well, knowing that faithfulness in even the smallest of callings will echo long into eternity.

Honest JOURNALING

Read through Colossians 3:1-17 and meditate on it.
In your journal, make a list of time-suckers in your life.
Which of these things don't really bring you
refreshment or aren't of eternal importance?
Which one can you cut down on each day or week?

3

Wise Use of Money

Lord, You say so much about money in the Bible because You know how big of a stronghold money issues can become. I do not want You to ever have to compete for my heart. Keep my security in You, not in our bank account. Everything that is done in secret will be brought to light (Luke 8:17), so I pray that our family manages our resources in such a way that we'd have no shame if the whole world were to see how we earn, spend, and give.

God, I pray for holy conviction regarding how our family makes money. May we bring a ministry mindset into whatever our hands find to do (1 Corinthians 10:31), conducting ourselves with integrity, even if it costs us financially. I pray for enough godly ambition to provide amply for our family's present needs without indulging, and for wisdom to prepare for the future without hoarding. Convict my heart if I am ever given over to greedy accumulation.

I pray for unity in our family. Let how we spend money be a conscious decision rather than an unguided habit. Lord, prompt me to be a cheerful giver, sharing financially wherever I see You working. I pray that money would not just be a piece of paper, but that I would regard both my time and my resources as ways to support Your work here on earth.

4

Give Me a Moldable Heart

Lord God, I pray for a moldable heart that is receptive to Your leading, Your teaching, and Your loving rebuke. You say in Your Word that a broken and contrite heart You will not despise (Psalm 51:17). There is a lot I have control over, but my heart is not one of those things. Only You can change my heart, so I ask for a heart that can hear Your reproof. God, criticism is never fun, but when I hear it, I pray for the strength of character to evaluate if what is said about me is true. May I never discount good counsel just because of who says it.

Lord, I pray for a heart that is growing daily in delight for the things that please You. And I pray to be resensitized to the things that grieve You; if something is contemptible to You, let it also be repulsive to me. Lord, if I have grown complacent toward the sin in the world, the themes in my TV shows and movies, may You return to me a godly sense of shock and displeasure at unrighteousness. Help me surround myself with things that uplift truth, purity, goodness, and all that is excellent and praiseworthy.

I pray You would reveal to me when I am participating in anything that increases hardness or numbness in my heart. May I have the boldness to remove those influences from my life. God, with every breath, I place myself back in submission to You, seeking to walk in a way that brings glory to Your name. Guide the decisions I make each day. I pray against any kind of pride that would puff me up, and may I see myself humbly and with sober judgment (Romans 12:3). Grant me, God, a heart that responds willingly to the hands of the Potter.

Honest STEP

Pay attention to the media you consume. Do you ever find yourself rooting for (or unbothered by) things that would grieve God's heart (such as wanting two characters who are married to other people to finally "get together")? Make it a litmus test for yourself: When you are unbothered by a display of sin in a television show, you should probably turn it off for the time being (or permanently). You may be surprised at what you are *unable* to stomach anymore once you remove it from your life or regular viewing.

5

Memory for What I've Learned

God, I pray for my memory. Things came so easily as a child, but now as an adult, it feels like my brain lost so much of what it used to be capable of. Lord, I pray that You would renew the neurons in my brain, strengthening them so I can remember the things I learn. I want to follow You, and I want to point my kids to Your words—but Lord, I need enough memory for it to stay with me. I do not ask this for the sake of feeling smart but for the sake of leading my children in godliness. You know every cell in my brain. Where there is atrophy, may I build up resilience. Where there is decay, I pray You would bring Your healing hand of restoration.

Where I am filling my mind with darkness, I pray for Your conviction and for Your light to dispel the dark. Lord, where I have disturbing or shameful memories that hinder me, I pray for forgetfulness. Where I have thoughts that need to be taken captive, I pray for a warrior spirit.

God, bless the activities I do to renew my mind in Your Word (Romans 12:2). And make Your Word stick with me so I can speak Your love, conviction, rebuke, and encouragement with wisdom in all situations.

Honest RESOURCE

I (Hillary) recommend the Bible Memory app. You can record yourself reciting verses and play it on a loop. Try memorizing an entire Psalm! Memorization is easier than you think, and it's a great way to hide God's Word in your heart. Start with Psalm 23 or 27.

6

Humility Without Being Crushed

Lord, we are called to humble ourselves before You (James 4:10), and I confess that I am not always as humble as I should be. I trust my own thoughts. I trust my own plans. I assume I am right and that others are wrong. Lord, I cannot truly love others without humility. I cannot receive Your grace without a humble heart, and I need Your grace, God. So I pray the scariest of prayers: Humble me without crushing me into oblivion. Only You know how to do that. Please chastise me in the way that I will hear, but I pray You will protect my heart from the roots of self-hatred that could accompany Your discipline. And if You could accomplish this without burning any bridges between me and others, I would be very grateful.

God, I also pray against false humility that tempts me to tear myself down and believe I'm less than I am. When I disparage Your creation, convincing myself that I'm stupid, worthless, ugly, or untalented, may I reject this false spirit of humility and embrace true humility. I want to receive Your kingdom as a little child, and I want to love others above myself. Make me meek and modest, and help me to choose behaviors that elevate others and point them to You. May I truly see every person I meet as more important than myself.

Honest EVALUATION

Which is your tendency: to disparage yourself or elevate yourself? If you struggle with false humility, practice receiving a compliment without deflection, incredulity, or embarrassment. Where you think you're pretty hot stuff, look for ways to praise others.

7

Self-Discipline

God, a body at rest tends to stay at rest, and I confess that I have allowed inertia to set in. Before I can even pray for self-discipline, I must actually *want* self-discipline—so please orient my desires toward that which will discipline my heart, body, mind, and emotions. Help me stick to a schedule that will encourage healthy, daily, rhythms, but also grant me the wisdom to know when to be flexible.

When it comes to food, I pray You would help me desire what is nourishing. I pray over my attempts at physical exercise, asking that You would make my body crave movement and fitness. I do not pray for fitness for fitness's sake, Lord, but that I would be a good steward of the body entrusted to me. I cannot serve others if my body cannot handle the load. So, for the sake of Your kingdom, give me an enjoyment of exercise, but also the knowledge and faith (yes, faith!) to rest when needed.

I pray for self-control when it comes to social media. May I use it for the purpose of connecting with others and not for zoning out. When it comes to my brain, Lord, I pray that I would not shy away from a challenge. Give me a love of learning that I can model to my children, especially when it comes to understanding You more.

I pray over the gifts and talents You've given me, that I would cultivate them to the best of my ability. Help me prioritize using my gifts for the sake of Your body, the church, and my family. There is nothing I have that was not given to me by You, oh God. May I seek to be a faithful manager of these gifts so that, one day, I will be proud to stand before You as one who has proven faithful to the task. I long to hear Your voice say, "Well done, good and faithful servant! You have been faithful with a few things…Come and share your master's happiness!" (Matthew 25:23).

(Review the Honest Step on the next page.)

Honest STEP

Research shows that it takes 30 days to form a habit. Pick one beneficial thing that takes 15 minutes or less, and try adding it once each day for a month.

8

Contentment with Just Enough

Lord, I sometimes think about what it would be like to have more. A bigger house, more money, longer vacations. I confess the spirit of discontentment that I have allowed to grow in my heart. In Romans, a spirit of ingratitude is at the head of all the chaos that comes after, and ingratitude is the gateway to wickedness (1:21-32). God, I pray that I would guard my heart and mind against ingratitude by intentionally cultivating a spirit of thanksgiving in our home.

I thank You, Lord, for not giving me more than You already have. The more I have in this life, the more *comfortable* I become with this life. As a Christian, I am supposed to feel like a foreigner in this world (1 Peter 2:11), for I am not yet home. God, forgive me for bowing to the idol of comfort as if it were evidence of Your favor. I *never* want to be so relaxed in this life that I wouldn't be willing to drop everything to follow You, because You *have bid me* come and follow. May my desire for earthly convenience never sway me from taking up my cross daily (Luke 9:23). So, Lord, I pray for enough resources to provide for my family, enough margin that I might give cheerfully, and just enough discomfort to remind me where my real home truly is.

Honest JOURNALING

What is an area of discontent that you struggle with? Why do you think you are prone to discontentment there? Write down three ways the Lord has been faithful in that area in the past. Then meditate on gratitude for the ways you've seen Him work.

9

A Life of Balance and Discernment

Lord, the Christian life can feel like a balancing act. What is wise in one situation is foolish in another (Proverbs 26:4-5). There is a time and a place for all things (Ecclesiastes 3:1-8). So, God, I pray for the discernment to know how to respond wisely in every situation.

Show me when to speak and when to be silent. Where a hug and encouragement are needed, give me the heart of a nurturer. But if a rebuke needs to be spoken, please show me how to phrase it graciously, as I hope others would do with me. When it comes to my children, God, help me to know when to build up and when to tear down (Ecclesiastes 3:3), when to encourage and when to correct.

Lord, it is easy to focus too much on the tasks You have given me at the expense of being still and listening to You. Please, God, impede my path wherever there is unhealthy striving, but neither let me coast along, mistaking complacency for faith. Show me when to step back and wait for You to slay the giant, and when to step forward in boldness to do what seems impossible.

God, some things come naturally to me, and some don't. I pray I would be diligent enough to invest in the strengths You have given me, yet humble and persevering enough to grow in the areas where I am weak. There is "a time to search and a time to give up" (Ecclesiastes 3:6). I pray You would clearly tell me when it is time to release things that are lost.

In my eating, in my sleeping, in my work, and in my play, I pray You would guide me in discernment, that I would model a life of balance. Give me the fortitude to remain untainted by the world, but also the willingness to go into the dark places where Your light needs to be shone. In all things, God, make me a representative of You—speaking, loving, acting, crying—being part of this world but not of it (1 John 2:16). I pray for balance in all things except radical obedience to Your commands, knowing that obedience to Christ *is* the path to the Father (John 14:4-6).

Stewarding My Body Well

Lord, You say in Your Word that our bodies are Your temples (1 Corinthians 6:19). I confess I have not kept Your temple the way I should. A thousand things vie for my attention, and taking the time to eat well and exercise keeps sliding to the bottom of my to-do list. It's the tyranny of the urgent, Lord. I pray for the diligence and self-control to steward this body to Your glory. I could ask for all the self-discipline in the world (okay, I ask for that too), but I know that more often than not, You work by *developing* our character rather than granting it. My motivation begins with my desires, so I ask, Lord, that You would change my desires.

I pray that I would crave and delight in the food that my body needs to be healthy. I pray that I would enjoy the process of exercising, and that working my muscles would bring me pleasure. I pray that when I eat right, my body would begin to crave that which is good for it and not enjoy that which would weaken it.

Father, please broaden my idea of what health looks like so I don't force my body into a size or shape it wasn't meant to be. I pray that as I age, I would accept my body's natural changes without shame or comparison. I thank You, Lord, for the laugh wrinkles, the stretch marks, and the gray hair, as they are evidence of joy and a life well lived (Proverbs 16:31).

God, I pray that I would see my stewardship of this body as another way to serve my family well. And for the areas over which I have no control—my genes, diseases, or chronic illness—I pray that I would rely on Your grace for the ability to do what You have called me to. May I never judge myself by what You have given to others. I thank You for this body, Lord, and all it can do. May I take the call to steward it well as seriously as I take every other calling in my life.

Honest JOURNALING

We women can be harsh on ourselves and our bodies, especially when we only focus on what we don't like or what isn't working. But there are so many things we take for granted, like being able to swallow, digest, lubricate our eyeballs, or walk. You don't know how thankful you are for these things until something happens and such simple abilities are gone. Make a list of all the things you are *grateful* about in your body. Also, evaluate which areas of your life have an unhealthy stronghold. Food? Exercise? Cosmetics or procedures? Social media filters? What is one thing you can do to be *kind and faithful* to this one body God has given you? Try it for 30 days (because that's how long it takes to form a habit).

Even small steps are better than no steps.

11

Prayer over Blind Spots

Lord, no matter how much I crane my neck, I'll never be able to see my own blind spots. But You are *El Roi*, the God who sees, so I ask You to use Your Spirit, Your Word, and the people You've placed around me to reveal the parts of myself I cannot see. Whittle away the obstacles that hinder my fellowship with You and with others, and pull back the defense mechanisms I've constructed to protect myself.

Open my eyes, Lord. I am blind and want to see. May the correction of Your Word bring me to perfect sight. And may I also remember that Your voice does not condemn; Your kindness leads me to repentance (Romans 2:4).

As I learn about myself, may I never use my "personality profile" to excuse my blind spots. I pray that You would bring people into my life who see what I don't, and help them graciously reveal it to me. I especially pray that I would have the ability to receive it well. Lord, may it be said of me that I am a woman who receives correction.

Honest STEP

Who is someone who knows you well, whose heart you trust to give you loving correction? Remind them regularly that they have permission to approach you (gently) about your blind spots. Practice gratitude for the people who take you up on the offer. Better are the wounds of a friend than the kisses of an enemy (Proverbs 27:6).

12

Healthy Identity

Lord, You made me, and You are the only one who can tell me who I am. Why do I keep looking to things of this world to define me? I am not my degree, my marriage, my job, or my kids. Oh Lord, I need reminding again today of what it means to place my identity in You:

I am Your creation, not the creator of myself. Nobody but You can declare the purpose for which I was created (Ephesians 2:10; Romans 9:19-22).

I am distinct from the rest of Your creation and more than just an animal. I was designed to rule over Your world in righteousness and justice. That was Your original plan in Genesis and Your final plan in Revelation (Genesis 1:26-28; Revelation 22:5).

You created me human: a physical, rational, emotional, and spiritual being (Mark 12:30).

I am an image bearer, made female in Your image, and You have called that good (Genesis 1:27, 31).

I was created for eternity, and this world is not where I'll be forever (Genesis 1:27; Matthew 25:46; 1 Thessalonians 4:13-18).

I am a sinner saved by grace (Ephesians 2:8-9). I am fallen but redeemed. I am imperfect but growing (2 Corinthians 3:18; 5:16-17).

I am not what I once was; nor am I what I one day will be (2 Corinthians 5:17). I am rational and, by God's power, am capable of ruling over my emotions, my hungers, my passions, and my fears (1 Corinthians 10:13; 2 Timothy 1:7).

I am grafted into the living vine (Romans 11:11-31). I can't help but produce spiritual fruit. I need not strive, and I need not strain. I need only abide in the One who causes all growth (John 15:1-5; 1 Corinthians 3:7).

I am a member of Christ's body, betrothed to Him and destined for oneness with Him. I put off, therefore, whatever belongs to my former nature (Ephesians 4:22-24; 5:30-32).

I am a unique part of His plan; nobody can play the part He has called me to play, and no other part of the body can call me dispensable. God has a redeeming purpose for my personality, my quirks, my skills, and my passions (1 Corinthians 12:21-26).

I am a mother of adopted, physical, or spiritual children. I lead as I am led. I nurture as I've been nurtured. I comfort with the comfort God has given me (2 Corinthians 1:4).

I am Yours, my Lord and my God. Irrevocably, unashamedly Yours. You are the eternal One, and You provide in Yourself my entire identity.

13

Prayer for Words

Lord, You spoke and pierced the darkness with Your marvelous light. Your words brought order out of disorder and created all that is good, true, and beautiful in the world. As Your Spirit inspired each stroke of the pen, Your earthly messengers inscribed Your words. I praise You, the Living Word.

While I don't possess the power to create something out of nothing, I recognize that the words I speak, write, or type have the capacity to provoke chaos or inspire calm. I know that just as a sculptor uses tools to chip away at marble to ruin stone or reveal a masterpiece hidden within, my words have the power to reveal either beauty or ugliness in my fellow image bearers.

I confess that I haven't always wielded my words with precision. I have been careless in both the timing and the tone with which I use them. I further confess that I have sometimes used technology to weaponize my words, celebrating mic drops or lobbing truth like a grenade. Like the psalmist, I implore You, Lord, to set a guard for my mouth and keep watch at the door of my lips (Psalm 141:3). May I use my words to daily speak encouragement over my husband, identity over my children, Your gospel over those around me, and truth over a dying world. Please let my words enhance the flavor of a life lived by grace through faith so I may gently and winsomely persuade others of Your glory.

Honest STEP

For people to receive our words well, we must build up emotional credit—a history of encouraging words. Identify a person whom you tend to criticize (or whom you notice may not get a lot of praise). Purposefully look for things in them to praise or encourage. Pour into them with your words, and watch how your mind begins to value them more as you look for good. Your words can bring life—not just for them, but for you as well.

Section 2

SPIRITUAL PROTECTION FOR THE HOME TURF

Parents' Bedroom

Lord God, I pray blessings over our bedroom, that it would be a sanctuary for my husband and me from the rest of the world. Peace in this home starts with peace in our marriage. Lord, may this be a room filled with love, romance, intimacy, unity, and bonding. I pray blessings over our marriage bed, that You would purge from us any desires that don't involve pure and sacrificial love for one another. I pray against any spirits of lust, anger, bitterness, or faultfinding. Any spirit that is not from You, Lord, I pray You would send it to the feet of Jesus.

I pray for Your rest in this room—that our bedroom would be a place of refreshment and recharge. I pray for the conversations that happen in the evening, that we would speak kindly and gently to one another. I pray for the spirit of unity, that we would continually seek oneness of mind, body, and heart.

Lord, let this room be a bastion of prayer, our war room before we enter the world. As we shed our clothes each night, may we each shed the cares of the day and the sins of our hearts. And as we get dressed in the morning, may we intentionally clothe ourselves in the armor of God (Ephesians 6:10-17). Lord, protect this room and protect our marriage. May we both submit to You in all things.

Honest HABIT

Establishing a bedtime routine can be difficult and a point of contention in marriages. However, the time you spend before you drift off to sleep is vitally important; Mom and Dad need to be checking in with each other. My husband and I (Hillary) make it a point to listen to a chapter on the Bible app each night and talk about it. We are making our way through the whole Bible. Afterward, we discuss what we are thankful for about that specific day (so each night it's something new). Then we pray either separately or together. Once you make this a part of your routine, you'll be surprised at how much you crave it when you don't do it! And if you are a Mama Bear with an unbelieving spouse, there are still things you can do. Stick with the points of gratitude for each day (as in the prayer "Reuniting with Husband After Work" on page 63), and remind your husband what you are thankful for about him every night.

15

The Single Mama Bear's Bedroom

Lord, You know the cries of my heart. Mama Bearing by myself is hard, but You have not left me alone. You say in Isaiah 54:5: "For your Maker is your husband—the LORD Almighty is his name." You are my only husband right now, God, and I cling to You all the more. I pray this room would be a place where I can cry to You openly. I pray it would be a place of intimacy between You and me, a space where I can confide both my fears and my delights to Your listening ear. I pray for Your spirit of peace in this room, that it may be a safe haven from all the burdens I carry. I pray this room will remind me to come before You with my joy and thanksgiving, mindful of all the ways You have provided for my needs.

When I walk through my bedroom door, may I remove every care and worry and place it at Your feet. I pray Your love would permeate my heart in a tangible way, so I may feel seen and heard and cherished and protected. I pray this room would be my war room, where I go to You in prayer for my children, and even for myself. Lord, increase my desires for You, Your Word, and Your presence here in this place. Be near to me, my God, for You promise to be near the brokenhearted and "those who are crushed in spirit" (Psalm 34:18). I praise You for all Your provisions and rejoice in the gentle kindness You show me morning by morning, evening by evening.

Honest HABIT

We were created for fellowship, and ending each night by praying with someone can be incredibly comforting. When I (Hillary) was single, I prayed nightly with a ministry partner. Is there another single (or unequally yoked) woman you know who might want to do the same?

16

Kids' Bedrooms

Lord, I pray for this room, that it may be a sanctuary for [child]. I pray Your presence would permeate and rule over every square inch. God, I pray against any spirits of fear, loneliness, bitterness, lust, or [things your child struggles with] that might try to influence [child]. God, place Your protecting angels at the door to this room, guarding it by day and by night. May every person who comes through this door be filled with Your peace.

I pray against any negative influences that would try to enter; may they be stalled at the door, unable to step foot inside. I pray against any spiritual "noise" that would prevent [child] from being able to hear Your voice here. May this room be a place where [child] can commune with You, [his/her] heavenly Father. I pray that [child] would discover [his/her] gifts and strengths here—that this would be a place for careful reflection and pondering of Your truths, of exploring imagination and creativity. I pray this room would offer rest and respite from the craziness of the world, and that it would be a fortress of calm in an often chaotic world. Lord, spread Your hand of protection over this room. You are *Yahweh Shalom*, the God of peace.

Honest EVALUATION

What are some particular things your child struggles with— and what good things could take their place? Ask for Him to pour out His spirit of peace if your child struggles with anxiety. If your child struggles with anger, pray that he or she would find the words to verbalize his or her frustrations. Laziness? That God would captivate him or her with a specific passion to use for God's glory, like drawing, reading, building things, or music. Remember: The more specific we can get in our prayers, the better.

17

Living Room

Lord, please protect and bless our living room, that it would be a place of family, friends, fun, and laughter. I pray against any spirits of discord, that this room would be a place of sweet fellowship.

I pray over the media that we consume in this room and that You would convict us if (or when) we are watching something that will erode our desire for holiness. Lord, we can't avoid everything in pop culture, so I pray for Your spirit of discernment to permeate this place. When the television depicts the world from an unbiblical perspective, help me and my kids to spot it and have fruitful discussion—separating the good from the bad, the wise from the unwise, and the truth from the lies.

I pray this would be a room of communion as we learn how to interact as a family and as hosts to guests. May the memories that are formed in this room, Lord, be wholesome and good, and may the lessons learned here be lasting. Oh God, I ask You to come and be present here today and every day.

Honest STEP
(repeated from Give Me a Moldable Heart)

Pay attention to the media you consume. Do you ever find yourself rooting for (or unbothered by) things that would grieve God's heart (such as wanting two characters who are married to other people to finally "get together")? Make it a litmus test for yourself: When you are unbothered by a display of sin in a television show, you should probably turn it off for the time being (or permanently). You may be surprised at what you are *unable* to stomach anymore once you remove it from your life or regular viewing.

18

The Digital Sphere

Lord, I pray for our family's use of the internet, screens, and social media. Please show us when giving [child] access to a device will be beneficial and when it will be harmful. We don't want to prevent the kind of learning that [his/her] peers are getting through interacting with technology, but neither do we want to impede [his/her] natural brain development by exposing [him/her] to more screen time than is healthy.

God, alert me to when [child's] physical or emotional health is being compromised by excessive use of technology. If or when that happens, may [his/her] father and I be willing to be the "bad guys" by taking it away. Please, God, let [child's] father and me be a united front. I pray for mutual agreement when it comes to our views about technology. Do not let any differences in perspective become a point of contention between us where [child] can play us against each other.

I pray for wisdom to know which apps to allow [child] to use and which to block. May we not bow to the whims of culture or popular opinion. Give us the words to articulate our reasons for not allowing [him/her] access so [he/she] doesn't think we are being arbitrary killjoys.

I pray that we adults would set a healthy example for responsible screen usage. May we never demand that our children be more disciplined than we are willing to be ourselves.

We thank You, God, for all the ways You bless us through technology. May we and our children know how to embrace the benefits without forming unhealthy addictions or habits.

Honest RESOURCE

Our kids are being exposed to *way* more screens than we ever were. We at Mama Bear Apologetics (MBA) recommend doing research on how screens are affecting kids' developing brains (like the documentaries *Screenagers* or *The Social Dilemma*). This will help you make informed decisions about screen rules and usage in your home.

Have you noticed a change in your kid's behavior? Lack of attention, focus, or patience? Maybe it's time for a total digital detox. We recommend the book titled (appropriately) *Digital Detox* by Molly DeFrank. (To hear an interview with Molly, check out Episode 74 of the *Mama Bear Apologetics* podcast).

19

Kitchen

Lord, I pray Your blessing over this kitchen, as it is our constant reminder of our dependence on You as our daily bread. I pray also that the food we eat here would be chosen thoughtfully and deliberately based on what *is* good, not just on what tastes good. (But Lord, let it be both!) We praise You for Your awesome gifts of fat and sugar; may we enjoy them in moderation. And I pray Your Spirit would release us from being slaves to food—whether too much or too little.

Lord, modify our taste buds to crave that which is nourishing for our bodies, just as You shape our character to crave that which is holy and pleasing. We thank You for the gift of food! As we prepare this meal, Lord, prepare our hearts. May we not resent the drudgery of the task but be thankful for what You have provided. Bless our time around the table; please make it a time of connection and not of contention. May the words we direct toward each other grow our family bonds and be pleasing to You.

Honest HABIT

Mealtime is one of the most precious times you have with your kids. As soon as you can, create a routine around mealtimes, establishing it as "family time." Take turns praying or write a family prayer that you all recite together regularly. At the close of the meal, make time for a short devotion or a Bible reading followed by a short discussion. These simple habits will help you reconnect as a family and remind your children to Whom y'all belong.

20

Grandparents' House

Lord, I thank You for the gift of extended family. Thank You that my children have living grandparents who love them. Abba Father, I pray over my parents' (or in-laws') house as my children and I spend time here. Let the time we share here be full of love and laughter, as generations come together to impart and receive wisdom. I pray that my children would be oblivious to any area of contention between me and my parents (in-laws), and that any old disagreements would be left at the door as we establish new relationships around this young generation.

Lord, I pray that Your wisdom would be spoken in this house. Please give my parents (in-laws) the joy of investing in my children and pointing them toward You and Your truth. If there are areas of ideological disagreement between my parents (in-laws) and us, I pray You would protect my children's minds from confusion. Then help us to address it with the kids later in a way that is fruitful and respectful of their grandparents.

I pray for grace as both my parents (in-laws) and I are learning to navigate these new roles with new boundaries regarding grandchildren. Help me to walk in humility as a vessel of Your love to my parents (in-laws), enjoying the days we have left with them. As far as it depends on us, may my husband and I model for our children a living example of what a healthy family should look like.

21

Child's Friend's House

Lord God, thank You for the gift of friends! I thank You that my child has relationships with other children, and I pray You would grow these friendships deeper and deeper. But God, I hear so many stories about things that happen at sleepovers or other visits to friends' houses. It makes me want to keep my children at home with me forever, but I know I can't do that.

So, Abba, I pray special protection over [child] as [he/she] goes to [friend's] house. Grant [him/her] a special helping of discernment. If anything unhealthy is going on, I pray that [child] would be able to articulate it to me without feeling like a tattletale. If there are siblings in the home, I pray for protection against any kind of bullying, abuse, or inappropriate behavior. I pray You would give [child] the where-withal to recognize if a situation is dangerous, the wisdom to remove [himself/herself] from it, and the boldness to speak if any boundaries were crossed. Lord, so many kids are introduced to pornography by a friend. I pray for malfunctioning technology if ever the friend or others in the house attempt to expose [child] to unhealthy content. Protect [child's] mind when [he/she] is away from the safety of our nest.

And Lord, as [child] invites friends over to our house, help us provide a cocoon of safety against the world for all who enter. I pray that I would be the Mama Bear to each of [child's] friends—protecting, advocating for, and investing in them as they spend time in our home.

God, You did not give me a spirit of fear, but of love, power, and a sound mind (2 Timothy 1:7). I give You the fears I have when my child leaves the home and is outside of my protection. May I prepare [him/her] well enough to face challenges, remain steadfast, articulate the truth, and lead others into the beautiful knowledge of Your goodness.

(Review the Honest Habit on the next page.)

_____

_____

_____

_____

_____

_____

_____

_____

_____

_____

_____

_____

_____

_____

_____

_____

_____

_____

_____

_____

Honest HABIT

When your child's friends come over, don't be shy about reminding *everyone* of the house rules. Your home might be the only place where your child's friends experience the security of boundaries. When your children go over to a friend's house, don't be afraid to ask the friend's parents about their house rules, and make sure your child clearly knows what is expected of him or her. Clarity is kindness, and rules are for protection.

FROM BZZZZ!!! TO ZZZZZ...

Short Prayers for the Daily Grind

22

Upon Waking Up

Oh Lord, my God, Maker of heaven and earth, I praise You for another day of life. You alone know what today holds. May I work cheerfully and with contentment, taking joy in the tasks You have put before me. Give me energy when I'm tired, joy when I'm stressed, and the eyes to see what is most important for the day. I invite You, God, into my every moment. "May these words of my mouth and the meditation of my heart be pleasing in your sight, Lord, my Rock and my Redeemer" (Psalm 19:14).

23

Before Waking Up the Kids
(and Chaos Ensues)

Lord, thank You for these little ones, whom I have the privilege of waking up each morning. I love the calm before the storm. Away goes my quiet, but awake comes my heart. Thank You for this new day of life with my precious children. Grant me patience to deal with whatever comes our way. Temper my words to be fitting for the moment. May all I do glorify You and show them Your love and character.

24

Prayer from Head to Toes

Lord, I pray for [person/child/spouse] from [his/her] head to [his/her] toes.

I pray over [his/her] feet; may [he/she] walk in ways pleasing to You—not departing to the left or the right (Proverbs 4:27).

I pray over [his/her] legs; may [he/she] have the strength to persevere through hardship.

I pray for [his/her] stomach; may [he/she] not be ruled by desires but by that which is pure, nourishing, beneficial, and life-giving.

I pray over [his/her] shoulders as [he/she] bears up under heavier burdens than [he/she] thinks [he/she] can hold.

I pray for [his/her] neck; may it not become stiff to Your reproach.

I pray for [his/her] head; may it be filled with light and truth, love and peace, and the knowledge of You.

25

Putting Kids on the Bus

Lord, I hand over my most precious packages to [bus driver]. I pray You would bless [him/her] for performing an often-thankless job. Lord, guide [bus driver] to be alert to traffic and what's going on in the bus. Give [him/her] immeasurable patience and authority to maintain control. Please deliver these children safely to their school, and thwart the attempts of anyone or anything that would dare try to harm them en route to or on campus.

(For bullying, see "When My Child Witnesses Bullying" on page 231 or "When My Child Is Bullied" on page 232.)

Honest STEP

Do you know your bus driver's name? If not, ask! Make it a point to call him or her by name! The driver may not receive many thanks. Tell him or her that you pray for them every day. You never know what kind of conversations it might open up.

26

Blessing over Quiet Time

Lord, I thank You for Your Word. I thank You that it is living and active, capable of molding my heart, mind, soul, and spirit (Hebrews 4:12). Please speak to me as I open these pages; instruct, correct, rebuke, encourage, equip, and give me hope. Even when the reading seems dry, remind me that I cannot leave Your Word unchanged. May every moment I spend in the Bible leave me with an insatiable longing for more. May my desire for knowledge about You be equally yoked with knowing You more.

27

Before the Tasks I Don't Enjoy

Lord, it's time for [task] again. I know I am to be thankful in all circumstances, so I thank You for [task] (1 Thessalonians 5:18). I know I am to do all things as unto the Lord, so may I never degrade any part of my job (Colossians 3:23). [Task] is no less glorifying to You than the larger or more enjoyable tasks. Help me rejoice in the smallness of these tasks, knowing my obedience is itself an act of worship. Oh God, I want to worship You in all things! So please, accept this small act of faithfulness as my way of singing Your praises. Reward me in this tiny act of submission by molding my character even more into the likeness of Your Son.

28

While Doing Laundry

Here it is again, Lord. More piles of dirty laundry. Land mines across my floor, behind the doors, even in the car. I get tired of the wash, rinse, and repeat multiple times per week.

Change my attitude, Lord. Help me see this task as a metaphor for what Your love and forgiveness does for me and my kids. Just as they wear different sizes and styles, help me sort out how to pray specifically for each of them. Help me remember how You treated the stains of my sins and washed me white as snow. Help me choose the gentle cycle when they need it. When my response needs reshaping, gently form me. When they need to air their dirty laundry, let them feel safe coming to me and to You. And as I ask them for the bazillionth time to put their things in the hamper (instead of on the floor), do not ever let them be hampered with unrepentance when they sin. The time will come when the only time I do their laundry is on trips home from college. Soon the baskets will be empty, and I will have no more clothes to pick up. This too shall pass. Let me not begrudge it but embrace it— even if it stinks for a little while.

Honest IDEA

Folding laundry doesn't demand too much brainpower. Use this time to either pray over your kids individually or listen to an educational podcast. And if you need somewhere to start, we've heard the ladies over at *Mama Bear Apologetics* have a pretty great one.☺
(Our totally unbiased opinion, of course!)

29

Before Driving

As I take the wheel, Lord, grant me alertness and freedom from distraction. Let me take seriously the machine I control and the lives that could be affected by how I handle it. May I never cause harm to another through my inattention or inaction. May any road rage come under self-control. Help me respect the law and officers of the law and set a worthy example for my children.

30

Preparing to Reengage with Kids

L ord, as I sit in the carpool line, use this time to refine me in the process of waiting. Help me take a breath and not be consumed by the unfinished things on my to-do list. Prepare me to interact well with my children as they climb in the car, excited or distressed about their day. May I show joy toward the things that excite them and compassion toward the things that have hurt them. Help me to patiently give them space if they need time to process their day silently. Alert me to anything unspoken on their hearts while still giving them the freedom to come to me in their own time, instead of forcing it out of them. When I have needs, may I clearly and gently verbalize them. My children are not mind readers. I pray that You would attune each of us to the needs of the other as we embark on the next phase of the day at home.

Honest PREPARATION

It's easy to scroll your phone while waiting for your kids to hop into the car, but this contributes to the noise in your brain. We all need quiet and stillness, and this is one of the few times you have it. Don't let it go to waste by multitasking. Revel in the solitude and quiet. And if you find it near impossible to be still, treat that as a sign that you *really* need to unplug.

31

Reuniting with Husband After Work

Lord, You are the foundation of this family. Our roles as husband and wife, mother and father, show our children who You are. As we come back together after a long day, I pray that we would still have time for kisses, compliments, and kindness. A solid marriage paves the way for secure and happy children. Lord, we release the troubles of the day, leaving them out on the doorstep. We consecrate this home as our haven against the world. May the frustrations we experienced today not come out on each other or on our children.

Honest HABIT

If possible, have whoever is coming home last give the other notice. Before you start the next phase of the day with the family, take a few quiet moments together as husband and wife instead of jumping right back into your roles as Mom and Dad. Repeat the above prayer (or a similar one) together. Then specifically say one thing you are thankful for about your spouse *that day*. Making it a daily gratitude will help keep it from being too general or repetitive. Share a kiss, and at *least* a 20 second hug. (Our bodies need a full 20 seconds to release the oxytocin!) Make sure the kids know this time is sacred for Mom and Dad. Anything else they want can wait until after Mom and Dad have reconnected. Also, finish any text or phone conversations *before* you walk in the door. Don't enter the house distracted.

32

Before Watching Entertainment

Lord, You are the author of beauty and laughter, and we praise You as the original artist. You are the great weaver of stories. As we sit down to enjoy this art and entertainment, may Your laws of goodness be ever before us. Sharpen our minds as we enjoy these gifts, so we may discern what is good and pleasing about this story and what is not. Where there are lies, please point them out. May we never grow desensitized to sin, and may we always crave the good things You have created.

33

Before Putting Kids to Bed

How can going to bed for one creature cause such misery when it's all *this* creature wants to do? Lord, please do not let tonight be another battle. I pray for patience when [child] keeps getting up. May I remember that I am the parent and [he/she] is the child. May I not give in to [child's] whims just because it is easier. May I be consistent with the little things so I need not wrestle as much with the big things. Please bless my child with a healthy exhaustion, and let each day end in sweet snuggles and sleepy kisses. And even when they don't, may I still count it all blessing to be the mother of this child.

34

Release at the End of the Day

Another day has come and gone, full of things I can no longer change. You alone, Lord, know what was really accomplished today. For the areas of success, I thank You for Your goodness. I pray that anything sown through my sin would be forgotten and that I would learn from my mistakes. Let the things sown from Your power multiply, echoing into eternity. Where I have erred or hurt others, show me how to repent and make amends.

I release this day to You, in good and bad, in triumph and defeat. But no matter how today has gone, tomorrow is another day, every morning renewed with Your mercy (Lamentations 3:22-23 NASB). Give me refreshing sleep, Lord, and as I wake up, remind me once again that each day's battle belongs to You (1 Samuel 17:47).

Honest ENCOURAGEMENT

Remember, the Lord is the only one who truly knows what was accomplished today. Even when you feel like you've just been a hamster on a wheel, things happened in the spiritual realm that you may not even be aware of. Sometimes even a nap is the most productive and God-glorifying thing you can do.

Section 4

FROM MY BEAN
TO MY BEAN'S BEAN
Ages, Stages, and Rhythms of Life

Pregnancy

Lord, thank You for the new life growing inside me. I am in awe of Your creation. The way You designed us to bring forth new life testifies to Your existence. You knew this child and the path for his or her life before I ever knew I was pregnant. I'm so grateful for Your guidance. You have blessed me with the role of mom, but this child is ultimately Yours. Remind me, Lord, that no matter the outcome, weight gain, or hormones, *You* are in control.

Refresh me, Lord, when moments of fear try to steal the joy of the moment. Help me see the beauty in my earthly temple as I foster this new life. It's so easy to feel inadequate, but my body is doing exactly what You designed it to. I don't have to meet worldly beauty standards because I already am precious in Your sight. Because of Your love, I will rejoice in what pregnancy does to my body and love each stage for what it is. Each stretch mark is worth the honor of being called "Mom."

Help me embrace the sacrifices needed to take care of my physical body while this baby is sharing my resources. Where I need to give up habits, foods, or desires that are not healthy for my child, help me do so with gratitude and not with resentment. If I need to continue those sacrifices after birth, give me the discipline to do so.

As labor approaches, I take comfort in knowing that this too shall pass. Give my healthcare team wisdom as they help me deliver this baby. Give me strength as contractions come. Ease my fears about labor. Your Word says that joy will come in the morning (Psalm 30:5), which is such a comfort as I get ready to push this human through a canal that feels far too small! And if Your plan is for this baby to enter the world by other means, help me to trust You. When things are toughest though, Lord, I know that You are with me.

Please bring comfort to my family during this process. Help them feel Your presence when they feel helpless, and provide Your divine patience when I need one more taco run…or pint of ice cream…Both sound great right now! Above all, may this pregnancy reveal to them Your wonder and power, as it has for me.

For the Adoptive Mama Bear

Abba Father, I do not take for granted that I can call You Father. Thank You for adopting me into Your family—and as a coheir with Christ, no less! I rejoice in my adoption into Your family as I rejoice in the addition of [child] to our family—our adopted child. What a gift! No matter what comes, our family is richer. Thank You for giving us the gift of adoption, to help redeem that which has been broken.

Oh God, we can't ignore that adoption here on earth often begins with loss, trauma, and tragedy. Please forgive me if I have focused so much on my own desires and joy that I have forgotten the sorrow that [child] has experienced (or will experience) by being removed from [his/her] birth family. [He/She] was separated from the only comforting heartbeat that [he/she] knew and thrust into the arms of strangers. But God, You created maternal bonding, and You can transcend it. I pray that Your power would supernaturally forge between us deep and lasting attachments that far surpass anything that was lost.

Teach me and grow me as an adoptive parent. Give me eyes to see and ears to hear the cries of [child's] heart. Protect my own heart from feeling rejected when [child] longs to know [his/her] birth family. All the love in the world cannot substitute knowing who [he/she] is and where [he/she] came from, especially in a world that so prizes individual identity. Help me to remember that when [child] seeks answers, [he/she] is not rejecting me, but simply wanting to understand [his/her] biological identity. Help me grieve [child's] losses alongside [him/her], not adding to [his/her] burdens, but being the adult who helps carry them. Grant me the patience to endure any of [his/her] difficult emotions without reacting from my own wounds or sinfulness. And as my husband and I shepherd this precious child who has experienced such loss, please protect our marriage from any added stress. May we approach each challenge as teammates.

Grant me empathy and wisdom to answer difficult questions about [child's] biological family in ways that are developmentally appropriate, gracious, and true. When [child] feels rejected, help me to point [him/her] to [his/her] true Abba Father to fill the emptiness.

In the chaos of understanding [his/her] identity as an adopted child, help [child] to experience the joy of being twice adopted—once by me and once by You. Give [him/her] a sense of eternal identity in Christ when [he/she] struggles with [his/her] human identity. Surround [him/her] with both our earthly family's love and the love of the family of God.

When [child] struggles to know where [he/she] belongs or how [he/she] fits into this world, remind [child] that [he/she] belongs first and foremost to You—which means it is natural to feel like [he/she] doesn't fit in with the world. Remind [him/her] that no matter the struggles [he/she] has endured, You will use all things for good of those who love You and are called according to Your purpose (Romans 8:28). Help us remember that [child] is Yours first and foremost. We are merely stewards of [his/her] life by Your grace. May we steward our precious little [child], reminding [him/her] daily that [he/she] is chosen and wanted by us. I thank You for being the God who creates beauty from ashes. And thank You again, God, for adopting me into Your eternal family.

To Not Screw Up My Toddler

Lord, You and [toddler] have something in common: Neither of you sleep! God, I need Your help. Should I even have expectations for a toddler? Give me meekness and patience with this mysterious and squirmy creature. [Toddler] is not at the age where [he/she] can understand my words or my actions, so help me not to expect more of [toddler] than [he/she] is capable of. Tune my interactions to [his/her] frequency. I feel like everything I do is being recorded as a core memory into [his/her] growing synapses, affecting [his/her] future ability to trust and feel safe. God, help me protect [him/her] when [he/she] can't even communicate [his/her] needs.

Lord, free me from this fear that every tiny mistake I make will become a permanent fixture in my baby's psyche; it's just not true, no matter what the enemy is whispering to me. When I reach my human limits, may I call upon the supernatural reserves that I've heard You give to new mothers. Please give me the wisdom and ability to know when I need to rest, and provide an affordable and qualified babysitter who can help out when I can't go on.

As I have forgotten the pain of childbirth, may my child forget all my mistakes as a learning mommy. I praise You, God, for making humans both resilient and forgetful in these young ages. Oh God, I am so tired. Please hold up my arms when I cannot hold them up myself (Exodus 17:12).

38

Children Exploring Independence

Thank You so much for the immense honor and blessing of being the mama to these beautiful children. Lord, please make Your presence known to these sweet little ones. As they are in situations that require independence, Lord, gift them the confidence to step out from Mom and Dad while still looking back for guidance. Show me when to step in and when to step back and release them, allowing experience to be the better teacher for the lesson. May I never impede their learning because of an overzealously protective instinct.

Lord, when my children's overconfidence puts them in an unsafe or unhealthy situation, please shelter them from any permanent harm. If I am distracted, may Your Spirit alert me to danger and prompt me to intervene. But most of all, help my children to understand the difference between defiance, rebellion, disobedience, and establishing God-honoring and developmentally appropriate independence.

39

For a Child with Separation Anxiety

God, help [child] to walk into school today without having to be carried like a surfboard again. Only You know if my back can handle another round of [him/her] flailing in my arms. Give [child] the peace only You can bestow, reminding [him/her] that [he/she] is safe in Your arms and in a classroom with kind teachers who care about [him/her].

Give me the patience and grace to reassure [child] when [he/she] is clingy, and help me not to lash out at [him/her] for [his/her] anxiety. Help me to understand where [his/her] fears are coming from and to offer [him/her] biblically rooted comfort and encouragement so [he/she] knows where her confidence and peace come from.

Help me to focus on what [he/she] needs and not on the opinions of onlookers as [child] transitions into the classroom today. Help [child] to know and feel that You are always with [him/her]. I ask for wisdom to know when to guide [him/her] through these moments step-by-step and when to back away, giving [him/her] the space to make that first move toward the door. Thank You for this beautiful child made in Your image. I need Your help to love [him/her] like You do. Though I may fail [him/her] sometimes, I pray that [he/she] knows that You never will, even when [he's/she's] forced to do scary things!

Honest IDEA

Explain to your child what a boomerang is and how it always comes back to you. Remind him or her that you are like a boomerang and will always come back. Maybe make a game out of saying that word when you drop off and pick up your child. "It's time for me to boomerang, sweet pea!"

40

Blessing over Children on Their Birthdays

To be read over each child on their birthday, with the whole family. Before you start, have each family member prepare to share what they love and appreciate about the birthday boy or girl.

Oh God, we thank You for [child]. [Child], you are precious to us every day, but we especially celebrate you on this day, your birthday.

We speak blessings over you, praying that you see yourself the way God sees you. We echo the delight He felt when He created you. May God bless you to know your true worth in Him so that your heart overflows with compassion, mercy, and love toward those around you. We praise God for the way He made you, knowing He decided in advance which gifts, skills, and interests would prepare you to fulfill His calling for your life. We rejoice as you discover who God created you to be, and we release you from our own ideas of who you should be or what your future should look like. As you grow up in our home and beyond, may we always steer you toward God's heart and truth and then release you to His plans—the plans He had for you before you were ever born.

We praise God for the gifts that we see in you, such as: [Have each family member list at least one gift, skill, or character trait they love about the birthday kid].

[Child], may God bless you to have wisdom in all situations, to know when to be a courageous warrior and when to be a compassionate healer. We pray blessings for you to recognize truth when you hear it and to reject the lies of the enemy. We are grateful for you as a member of our family—a member who belongs, who is loved, and who will always have a home with us. We pray that you never crave the praise of others because you have known what it means to be fully accepted right here in this home and before God.

[Child], may the Lord bless you and keep you. May He make His face to shine upon you. May He be gracious to you and give you peace (Numbers 6:24-25). And may you use the blessings we speak over you this day to turn around and bless the world, making the name of Jesus beautiful in the eyes of those who do not know Him. Blessed be the name of the Lord for creating you, our precious [child].

41

Kid's Party Stress

Lord, I need a moment. A reset of perspective. Kids' parties have gotten so out of hand, so over the top. Some people seem to spend a year's salary on just a party—the invitations, the decorations, the venue, the games, the themed food, and the favors for the guests! God, I feel like if I don't try to outdo the other moms, then my child will feel like I don't love [him/her] as much. This isn't healthy. This party has become more about me than [child].

Help me get my priorities right in throwing this party before I throw a tantrum of my own. Help me refocus on celebrating my child's life and accomplishments in a delightful and God-honoring way that also manages my child's expectations for the future. I pray for a day of fun and laughter for us both. May we be making cherished memories for the future, even on a budget.

42

Before a Family Trip

Lord, we pray for Your protection as we leave on this trip. Thank You for the gift of family. When we are tempted to argue, may we instead laugh and make memories. When we're tempted to criticize or speak sarcastically, may we bless, encourage, and uplift. Each trip we take is a once-in-a-lifetime opportunity to get to know and enjoy each other. Please bless us with safety, closeness, love, and patience. We invite You to be present with us today. May we have fun in ways that bring You delight, and may we enjoy You by enjoying each other. May the memories we make on this trip be reminisced about for decades to come.

Honest AWARENESS

The enemy loves sowing discord when the family is together. If you find yourself or your kids starting to get cranky and squabbly please see the prayer, "When Everyone Is at Each Other's Throat," on page 138.

43

Parent-Teacher Conferences

Here we go again, Lord. I have a love-hate relationship with these meetings. My hands can get sweaty, and my stomach can churn—you'd think *I* was the one going to the principal's office.

As I meet with [child's] teacher, I pray for a spirit of mutual respect and understanding for the roles we both play in [child's] education. Would You help us listen well to each other as we voice affirmations and concerns? Tear down any defensive walls we have built so we can come together for the good of [child]. Help each of us to speak and hear hard things with objectivity and compassion. May our common goal—the education and well-being of [child]—be the uniting force between us.

Even if I don't like this teacher, what [he/she] says, or how [he/she] treats my child, help me to verbally encourage and affirm the good I do see in [him/her]. Keep me cognizant of [his/her] time and the other parents waiting behind me. I pray for discretion and confidentiality to be kept sacred. Guide me as I share with [child] the results of the conference—good and hard—and help [teacher], [child], and me to work together to fix any issues that need to be addressed.

Honest REMINDER

Picture yourself with 30 kids in a room, each with different needs, and each with a supervisor holding you accountable to remember each need. That is what being a teacher is like. Remember to encourage your teacher at least twice as much as you express criticism (if not more!).

44

School Decision

God, give our family the wisdom to make the right decision about the kids' schooling. I don't like what I hear about what's being taught in the schools. I don't like the behavior I am seeing tolerated, and I don't like the values being promoted. Oh God, please guide us.

I feel so scared that You will call me to homeschool. And if You do, let me remember that You don't call the equipped; You equip the called. If homeschool is where You are leading us, please help me face my fears and find a co-op. Provide me with a community of like-minded Mama Bears who are serious about education, critical thinking, and preparing children for the world, not sheltering them *from* the world.

Lord, I'm not sure if we can afford private school. But if a Christian school will make the difference in my child's physical or spiritual well-being, then I pray You would show our family what we need to do to make it happen. I know that Christian schooling will *never* replace their father or me as the primary educator and spiritual leader. May we not use Christian schooling as a crutch or an excuse to disengage, but rather see it for what it is: another resource to fortify what we are already teaching our kids.

Lord, if public school is our only option, then I'll need Your help to prepare my child. Show us how to double up on spiritual armor. I pray for the wisdom and empowerment to teach my children to interpret reality according to truth and not the spirit of the age. May You open my children's eyes to the lies of culture as I seize every learning opportunity to reinforce objective, biblical discernment.

Whatever sacrifices we need to make, I pray we would do so joyfully, knowing we are investing in something far greater. God, where resources are limited, provide where we are lacking.

I know this is not a one-size-fits-all decision, nor are we bound forever to the decision we make this year. God, I pray that You would show me if my different kids need different solutions, and give me the bandwidth to do whatever is best for each child. Show me whose educational or social environment is not working, and give me the flexibility to change course when needed.

I know our decisions are based upon what *You* are calling us to do. Lord, I release any judgmental feelings I may have for the decisions other families make. You, God, have made us responsible for our own family, and our friends are responsible for theirs. Help us to support one another—not shame each other—for our respective schooling decisions. Let us each steward our families according to Your direction and not in reaction to peer pressure, fear, or whatever is easiest. There is no earthly investment more eternal than these children. God, help us to make the right decision each year for their schooling, and to do what will best mold their character and prepare them for the future.

45

Pubescent Identity Crisis

Lord, have mercy; puberty is here, and we're already in the thick of it. Help me remember what it was like for me during this time, and give me an extra dose of grace for [child's] unpredictability while not allowing bad attitudes to escalate and solidify. Help me delight not only in the child [he/she] was, but in the [man/woman] [he/she] is becoming. Allow me to revel in the mystery and beauty of [child's] transformation, affirming the good at each step.

God, I pray that I can roll with the chaos as [child] learns who [he/she] is. An athlete? An artist? A musician? Introvert? Extrovert? I pray that I would keep my mouth shut as I watch [him/her] experiment (appropriately) with clothing and hairstyles, knowing that this is part of the teenage discovery process. Help me give [child] the freedom to explore different parts of [his/her] personality, and help me journey along with [him/her], not belittling the process even when I think it's dumb.

God, where sin or lies are tampering with [his/her] God-given identity, let me be ferociously protective. But also Lord, help me see when a healthy exploration has turned into an unhealthy cry for help, attention, or an over-identification with the wrong crowd. Give me the wisdom to distinguish between harmless experimentation and harmful ideologies that seek to change [him/her] at [his/her] core. Show me when to allow [child] to make mistakes and when to remove [him/her] from dangerous influences. Give me the willingness to face [him/her] when I need to step up as the parent instead of always trying to be [his/her] friend. Please surround me with godly community who will encourage me if or when I need to make tough decisions.

Oh God, I need Your direction as I guide this precious child into adulthood. Don't let me sweat the small stuff, but please, please, Father, give me the wisdom to see when [child] is questioning the big stuff.

There are so many voices in our culture, especially on social media, that are telling [child] who [he/she] is apart from You. I pray for open communication with [child] as [he/she] decides which parts of [himself/herself] are open to interpretation, and which—as a follower of Jesus—are not. This is also a time when [he/she] is deciding whether being a Christian is who [he/she] really is or wants to be. May the truth we have imparted to [child] from [his/her] youth carry [him/her] through these uncertain years of change and discovery. I pray You would show [him/her] Your faithfulness and goodness in all situations, so that [he/she] knows that [he/she] can always return to You, no matter how far [he/she] has strayed.

Oh God, give me wisdom to shepherd [child] during this hormonal roller coaster. Help me to withstand the ups and downs, highs and lows. I never know which version of my kid is going to show up on any given day. I pray that You would parent *me* as I try to parent [him/her] through this beautiful but difficult season.

Honest CONVERSATION

There are a lot of unhealthy messages telling kids that if they feel uncomfortable in their body, then that means they are somehow "different" and need to discover their authentic selves. We think the opposite is true. If you loved puberty (and your changing body), *you* were the weird one. Before your kids reach puberty, tell them that it is basically part of their job description to be uncomfortable in their bodies for about eight years. Make sure they expect the awkwardness and discomfort so they aren't thrown by it when it comes. Maybe show them some especially awkward photos from your adolescence and remind them, "We've all been there."

46

Popping the Christian Bubble
Before the Kids Leave the House

Lord, as strong as [child's] faith may seem now, [he/she] is still in the proverbial greenhouse, waiting to step out into the jungle. Lord, protective Christian bubbles can be helpful for a time, but they cannot (and should not) last forever. And when they pop, it can be devastating for young people whose faith lacks reason or depth. So, God, I pray You would pop that bubble before [child] leaves our home.

God, please gently challenge [child] in [his/her] faith while [he/she] is still under our roof. I pray [he/she] would ponder the tough questions of Christianity and then bring them to me, [his/her] father, or [his/her] pastor. Please prepare us with satisfying answers that will help [him/her] to build a lasting faith that can withstand the storms of this world or the intellectual objections of a skeptic. Provide wise counselors in [child's] life who have emerged victorious from periods of suffering or doubt so that [he/she] knows that [his/her] faith can also withstand the dark nights of the soul. Lord, protect my child from unnecessary doubts, but do not let [him/her] reach adulthood thinking the Christian life is simplistic or easy; I do not want [his/her] faith to be shaken by the harsh realities of this world. May we do the hard work now in order to bypass future doubts.

I especially ask that [child] would have a personal encounter with You, the living God, and that [his/her] faith would never be just a dead set of dogmas passed down from parent to child. I pray that [his/her] Christianity will be one that [he/she] has actively wrestled through, not just passively accepted. May [he/she] have real, gritty conversations with You, Lord, because that means [he/she] is going to You when things are difficult. Lord, let us expose [him/her] to just enough lies of the world that [he/she] can tell the difference between true and almost true. By the time [child] leaves our nest, may [he/she] have a long track record of receiving solid answers to challenging questions. God, I pray that we would not fear exposing [him/her] to the tough parts of the faith, but would prepare [him/her] to face this world head-on—standing on a firm foundation that has been tested and found reliable.

Honest STEP

Growing up, my pastor's wife had a saying: "I don't want my children hearing about anything that they haven't heard in my kitchen first." Wise words, indeed. When kids encounter tough questions on their own without hearing about it from us, they assume *we've* never heard the objection before—or if we have, we can't answer it. Our aim is to address the tough questions while our kids are still interested in the truth of Christianity. How do we do this? First, be the one to introduce the questions or challenges. Or, if your kids are already asking questions, keep track of the questions as they come. (We recommend keeping a list on your phone so you can record the question immediately, no matter where you are when your kids ask it.) Second, dedicate regular time to discussing these tough questions as a family. Make sure to do your homework first though! For resources, see mamabear apologetics.com/resources.

47

Releasing My
Almost-Adult Children

Heavenly Father, the time from toddlerhood to teenager went too fast; now I find myself on the brink of launching my children into adulthood. I often long for the days of naps and never-ending snacks, and especially the certainty that my children were safely within the four walls of our home. Now I find myself crying out to You in new ways as they drive solo down busy streets and tackle important decisions on their own. I struggle with feelings of anxiety and fear. Have we done enough? Are my children prepared enough?

Oh God, I cry out to You for their safety and protection. Please help me as I learn to navigate this new stage, holding on lightly and not too tightly, reminding me that they are Yours. Above all, I pray they will remain anchored in Your truth, Your love, and Your promises, growing closer to You each day. Lord, help me to release [children] to Your care, trusting in Your plans and purposes for their lives. And after my children are grown and gone, may You feather this empty nest with happy and precious memories.

48

Adult Children to Walk Faithfully with God

Father, I did my best to raise my children up to know and love You. I've disciplined them when they needed it, just as You have disciplined me. But I know they are now responsible for their own choices—and the consequences of those choices.

My adult children face the same temptations today as Adam and Eve faced in the garden: to take their eyes off You long enough to doubt Your love and goodness, and therefore Your instructions. I pray for moral strength as their flesh constantly cries out to be satisfied by temporal enticements which the enemy dangles in front of them. The world lures them with appealing ideologies, calling them to conform to the moment while offering nothing of eternal value. I pray that my children would have a deeper and more abiding love for You than they do the quickly fading things of this world.

Father, please surround my adult children with a community of believers who will encourage them in their walk with You, and may they also be encouragers in return. Please surround them with mature believers who will hold them accountable to Your perfect moral law. Give them a demonstrable love for others in both word and deed. And may the seeds that I planted in their childhood yield beautiful fruit for generations to come.

49

Children's Future Spouses

Lord, I pray over [child's] future spouse. I pray that my future [son-in-law/daughter-in-law] will see strong and godly marriages modeled by parents, extended family, or family friends. Please allow [him/her] to witness what it looks like to compromise, persevere through difficulties, and relate to others with love and respect. I pray for ample opportunities for my child's future spouse to practice both humble apologies and gracious forgiveness. I pray that You would protect [his/her] sexuality and convict [him/her] when [he/she] is tempted to compromise. Build up [his/her] muscles of self-control so [he/she] will become a strong, faithful [man/woman] of God.

Lord, I pray that [he/she] will have many loving mentors who correct [him/her] quickly and compassionately when [he/she] is caught walking in arrogance, pride, or rebellion against Your Word. Please protect [him/her] from the lies of worldly temptation and keep [him/her] from forming sinful habits that might harm [his/her] future marriage. I pray that [he/she] will learn to love Your Word, joyfully submitting to its commands, and living out [his/her] identity in You.

I pray that You would instill within [him/her] a godly ambition, prioritizing responsible decision-making that will fortify their future family. Lord, grab their hearts and don't let go. Surround them with godly friends who will journey with them toward becoming a strong [man/woman] of God. Develop [his/her] spiritual gifts so that one day [he/she] can utilize them in serving a family.

I give You all my expectations of what my future [son-in-law/daughter-in-law] will look like, what kind of background [he/she] will come from, or what kind of interests [he/she] will have. I pray that [his/her] love for my child will only be exceeded by their love for You. God, protect [his/her] heart so [he/she] can enter a loving marriage with as few scars as possible—able to trust, able to love, and able to live in a respectful and understanding way.

FOR A DAUGHTER'S FUTURE HUSBAND

Lord, I pray that my daughter finds a husband who has learned how to lead with humility and gentleness. I pray that he will continue developing his skills in leadership by first seeking to serve. I ask that he cultivates a healthy respect for authority so he knows how to behave both *in* and *under* authority. Help him become a strong protector while staying tender enough to comfort a crying child. May his character and integrity flow from intentional decisions and not just unconscious habits, making it easy and natural for my daughter to respect him. As he pursues his career, let him prioritize providing for his family, while not neglecting his passions and talents. May he be preparing himself for a job that brings him joy. Give him a teachable spirit, and help him be humble enough to accept wise corrections. Develop his courage, growing him into a man who is brave enough to lead his family in truth, even when that truth is unpopular.

FOR A SON'S FUTURE WIFE

A woman of valor, who can find? (Proverbs 31:10). God, I pray for my son's future wife, that You would protect her from abusive authorities, for her own sake and for her future ability to trust my son. Give her the grace to understand my son and support him. When he shares his hopes and dreams, may she be an encouragement to him. Teach her to keep a peaceful home, providing my son with a sanctuary from the world (Proverbs 17:1; 21:9). I pray that she would embrace her God-given femininity, knowing it does not limit her in any way. May she have the work ethic of Martha, the thirst for learning of Mary, the courageous conviction of Jael, the prayerfulness of Esther, and the wisdom of the Proverbs 31 woman. I pray she would live in such a way that he is proud to have her as his teammate. May she be sensitive to the needs of those around her, bold enough to correct my son when he is wrong, and yet submissive enough to trust his leadership.

50

To Be a Good Mother-in-Law

God, my nest might be empty, but my heart is still full of love for [child] and the spouse [he/she] chose. Help me adjust to my new role as a mother-in-law. As [child] and [his/her] new family forge their own path, let me not stand in the way or try to redirect their plans. I pray that they will follow the biblical mandate to leave and cleave, while also choosing to stay connected with [his/her] father and me. May my child take the good [he/she] has witnessed in our lives and multiply it in [his/her] own, but keep [him/her] from repeating any of our past failures. I ask that [his/her] father and I not be grieved over their life choices. However, should that time come, enable us to sit back and allow natural consequences to be a teacher. Give us wisdom to know if we should intervene.

As I learn how to operate within my new boundaries as mother-in-law, show me how to be useful without being taken advantage of and without being overbearing. As tightly as I zippered my kids' jackets against the cold when they were little, help me now to zipper my mouth against un-asked-for advice. Help me to show concern and interest without prying. If we offer any financial help, may it not enable bad choices or create dependency. May [his/her] father and I be the parents You have called us to be long after [child] has left our home and formed a family of [his/her] own. And should we be blessed with grandchildren, may we take the wisdom we gained as parents and use that to grandparent even better than we parented.

Section 5

FROM CLAY TO VESSEL

Prayers for My Kids' Spiritual Formation

51

Child's Salvation

Father, I desire for [child] to grow up in the fear and admonition of You. I desperately want [him/her] in [his/her] Father's house at a young age—just as Jesus was. I pray You would save [child] as soon as [he/she] can recognize the need for a Savior; I pray that [he/she] can walk with You all the days of [his/her] life, never remembering a day when [he/she] didn't follow You. Save [child] by transforming [his/her] heart of stone into a heart of flesh.

Only Your Holy Spirit can accomplish this. I recognize I am not the author of their salvation story; You are. Help me trust You, the author and perfecter of faith. Forgive me when I try to bring about my child's salvation storyline by my own means. No catechism, Sunday school, or Bible memorization can save [him/her] without Your Holy Spirit. Help me trust Your timing as well, Lord. For even if You change [his/her] heart later in life, I thank You still for Your tremendous grace.

Save [child], I plead. Living Word, inscribe [his/her] name in Your Book of Life.

52

Child to Develop Personal Faith

Father, I pray You will help [child] develop a personal faith relationship with You. Not a hand-me-down faith that [he/she] "puts on" just because we "gave it" to [him/her] through church attendance. May [he/she] clothe [himself/herself] in righteousness through a salvation experience that is true, genuine, and unique.

I pray for [child] to grow in spiritual wisdom and godly stature as [he/she] learns to study the Word for [himself/herself]. May [child] learn to seek and find You through prayer and have a will that is conformed to Yours. Wrap [child] in fellowship and accountability within a theologically sound and spiritually robust local church that is committed to love and service. And then, Lord, may that cycle repeat itself through future generations of our family.

Honest RESOURCE

Research says that one of the best things we can do to help our children develop a lasting faith is to disciple them in Bible study methods and personal prayer. It's never too early to start! Give each of your children their own age-appropriate Bible and prayer journal and teach them how to practice spiritual disciplines on their own. We recommend Foundation Worldview's "Studying the Bible" curriculum. You can find it at www.foundationworldview.com.

53

Kids to Love the Word

Father in heaven, more than [child] desires [his/her] favorite toys and TV shows, more than friends and social media, more than the acceptance and approval of others, more than anything in life—create in [child] an insatiable desire to know You through Your Word.

May [he/she] study, memorize, and meditate on Your truths so that [he/she] is prepared to share it with others. Never let [child] get tired of, grow bored with, or assume in arrogance that [he/she] knows all there is to know about You or Scripture. Give [him/her] a thirst for learning and the humility to change [his/her] theology when it is in contradiction to Your Word. But most of all, may [child's] character, behavior, and attitudes be transformed by Your Word. Let Your kindness, patience, joy, peace, truthfulness, and love overflow out of [him/her] as [he/she] abides in you, the true vine (John 15:1-8). I pray that the other kids around [him/her] will experience Your loving-kindness through [him/her], and so be drawn to Your Word as well.

Honest HABIT

Memorizing Scripture is helpful for everyone. And don't limit yourself to single verses—pick longer passages. It helps to understand the verse in context. Pick a passage to memorize each week and post it around the house. (Maybe introduce the passage for the week every Sunday night.) Challenge yourself, your kids, and your husband to memorize together.

54

For Children to Love the Church

Heavenly Father, thank You for the church. Despite its flaws and imperfections, I pray my child would trust Your plan for the church and always be committed to a local body of believers—a community committed to truth, love, and obedience to Your Word. May [he/she] crave the fellowship and encouragement that can only be found in a community dedicated to following You.

Please provide trustworthy shepherds in [child's] life who will point [him/her] to Christ. You alone are the perfect Shepherd, and You promise to guide all Your children through green pastures, beside quiet waters, and even in the valley of the shadow of death (Psalm 23:1-4). While many human leaders strive to follow Your example, I know that often they fail to shepherd others according to Your perfect ways. Please protect [child] from any leaders who would abuse their authority, whether intentionally or otherwise, and especially guard [child] from any spiritual leaders who are misusing Your Word for their own ends.

Give [child] wisdom and discernment as [he/she] participates in the church's mission. Help [him/her] to vigilantly protect their church body with sound doctrine, and give [him/her] eyes to recognize when compromise or coldness is sneaking in. May [he/she] stand against the wicked schemes of those who would attack Your church, whether from inside or outside the walls (Acts 20:29-30).

Help [child] to find friendship and fellowship as [he/she] discovers which gifts You have given [him/her] for the edification and building up of the church (1 Corinthians 14:12). Guide [child] to love and support the people and the ministries of the church through prayer, deeds, and words of affirmation. Allow [him/her] to have healthy experiences in church that reveal the beauty of the gospel message and encourage [him/her] to stay rooted in a faith community for a lifetime.

Honest CONVERSATION

With as much abuse as we hear about going on in churches, we need to reinforce early and often that the truth of Christianity is not dependent on Christians, but upon the life, death, and resurrection of Jesus. Do not hide the blemishes of the church, but remind your kids that church is full of imperfect people (and even wolves). Teach them to distinguish between Christianity and Christians so that a bad church experience does not rock their faith.

55

Fostering Gratitude and Contentment

Lord, I pray for godly contentment in [child]—a virtue that can only come through gratitude. It is so hard when [his/her] friends are getting things we cannot afford. My child may not have the best of everything, but [he/she] has everything needed for life, godliness, and good works (2 Peter 1:3; 2 Corinthians 9:8). I pray that [he/she] would not compare [his/her] own situation against [his/her] peers or covet that which is not [his/hers].

Bring it to [child's] attention when others have less than [he/she] does; may [he/she] see it as an opportunity to practice generosity. I pray You would give [him/her] the eyes to see the non-tangible gifts You have provided: a loving family, safety, security, and a peaceful home with parents who love [him/her]. Not every child can say the same. May [he/she] value what You value and only yearn for that which will aid in advancing Your kingdom.

Honest HABIT

Before bed every night (or at the dinner table), have each person say what he or she is most thankful for that day.

56

Healthy Outlets for Emotions

Lord, being a kid is hard. Little people can have big emotions and lots of them. Help me to be patient as I teach [child] to identify [his/her] emotions and then choose healthy outlets to express them. Our culture platforms and applauds people who spew their every feeling, equating emotional outbursts with "speaking truth." I pray that [child] would feel comfortable expressing [his/her] feelings without erupting into emotional rants.

Help me coach [child] to identify what emotion [he/she] is feeling and why so that [he/she] can respond appropriately and productively. I pray I would help [child] channel [his/her] emotions in a healthy way, reminding [him/her] that the best art, the most beautiful songs, and the fiercest athletes are often the result of passions directed toward constructive ends.

Give me the eyes to see when [his/her] behaviors are hiding big feelings that [he/she] doesn't know how to express. I pray especially over frustration, as this one emotion can be the root cause of many behavioral issues. As [child] learns to identify [his/her] emotions, may [he/she] use this knowledge to develop healthier coping mechanisms. I pray that this introspection would not lead to self-preoccupation, but rather to a greater sense of self-control and the ability to empathize with others.

Lord, I say all this as I look in the mirror. I can sometimes let my own emotions get overrun by my child's emotions, and then I find myself modeling all the things I'm trying to teach [child] *not* to do. Please grant me grace and levelheadedness to be the example I want [him/her] to follow.

57

When Kid Makes a Big Mistake

Oh Lord, [child] is embarrassed. [He/She] has [state the big mistake the child has made] and doesn't know what to do about it. Lord, may this be the beginning of [child] getting to know You as the one who can restore all things. Help [child]—in whatever capacity [he/she] is able—to admit where [he/she] has failed and why; help [him/her] to be honest about how [his/her] actions contributed to the problem and then own up to the consequences. Use this uncomfortable lesson for [child's] sanctification.

Help me teach [child] to approach Your throne with confidence and without fear, so that [he/she] may receive mercy for [his/her] failures (Hebrews 4:16). And may [child] know me as a safe place where [he/she] can confess [his/her] mistakes instead of hiding them. Please do not allow fear of disappointing me to prevent [him/her] from admitting when [he's/she's] in trouble. Please allow [child] to trust me with [his/her] heart, even when [he's/she's] messed up big-time.

And as I help [child] deal with the fallout, may I reflect Your grace and forgiveness while encouraging [him/her] to reach out to those [he/she] has harmed, making amends and righting whatever damage [his/her] actions may have caused. Thank You, God, that You can use even our failures for Your glory. I pray that this lesson, though painful, may result in giving [child] wisdom for the future and compassion for others when they make big mistakes.

Discerning God's Voice
from Other Voices

Oh Lord, the world is so loud, sometimes even deafening. [Child] is bombarded with so much information, much of it distorted by lies. Getting distracted from the truth of Your Word is becoming easier and easier amid the clamor and chaos. God, help [child] to discern the difference between Your voice and the voices of those influenced by the enemy or unhealthy worldly perspectives. Keep [child] mindful of the deceiver's tactics, and constantly remind [him/her] to test every message [he/she] hears against the truths of Scripture, reason, and reality. Help [him/her] know that the battle for discernment isn't always between overt good and evil, but as Charles Spurgeon said, "between right and almost right."

Lord, the enemy wraps his most potent lies in partial truths. Protect my child from believing deceptions that sound good, loving, and even Christlike though they ultimately lead to death. Keep [child's] heart tuned into Your voice, knowing that You are always at work even when You seem silent.

For Child's Sin to Be Exposed

God, no beating around the bush here: If my [child] is sinning, please expose it. If [he/she] is heading down a dangerous road, please let [him/her] get caught—*every time*. Please provide people around [child] who are bold enough to tell me if they see problematic behavior. I pray for keen Mama Bear instincts that would alert me to sin in the camp before the behavior gets out of control. I pray that [child's] conscience would kick into overdrive, and that [he/she] would exhibit unmistakable, telltale signs of a guilty conscience when [he/she] knows [he/she] is doing wrong.

Most of all, I pray that the outcome of being caught would be [child's] correction and restoration. I pray that I would faithfully correct this behavior while [child] is still under my charge so that future authorities do not have to do the job I should have already done. Please show me how to pick my battles, and may I never turn a blind eye to sin because I'm too tired to deal with it. When discipline is needed, I pray that You would give me the insight to know which punishment will be the most effective for this particular child. When there are natural consequences for [his/her] actions, may I resist the impulse to swoop in and protect [him/her] (Ecclesiastes 8:11). Most of all, may [child] develop [his/her] own moral conscience so that [he/she] doesn't need to be caught in order to repent.

Reconciliation and Forgiveness When Hurt

Father, I pray for [child]. [Child] has a heart for You, and I am so thankful for that. But [he/she] is having trouble with [person]. There is hurt from the past that is preventing [him/her] from truly forgiving [person]. This scar can only be healed by You.

Please help [child] to first examine [himself/herself] honestly and see where [he/she] has any fault in the matter. Compel [him/her] to admit [his/her] mistakes and turn from any areas where [he/she] has been at fault. I pray that healthy conviction—rather than shame-filled condemnation—would cause [him/her] to repent, seek forgiveness, and also to forgive [himself/herself]. Let [child] do what [he/she] can to seek peace over this issue with [person], remembering that we are all fallen. Help [child] to see that [he/she] can only be responsible for [himself/herself] and not [person's] response or reaction.

Give [child] the ability to release this hurt and to move forward. Help [him/her] to set appropriate boundaries while still extending grace and mercy to [person]. As far as it depends on [him/her], let [child] live at peace with others (Romans 12:18). If it be Your will, Lord, we pray for complete reconciliation between [child] and [person].

Honest EVALUATION

It is easy to point the finger at what other people have done to us. When we are hurting, it can be helpful to remember times when we—whether intentionally or unintentionally—have hurt others. Doing so helps us extend mercy to others who have hurt us. Make sure to pray honest blessings over the person who has hurt you or your child.

61

Cultivating Sexual Faithfulness

Heavenly Father, my precious child is coming of age in a time when puberty and sexuality have never been more confusing. I feel woefully unprepared for the things [child] will have to face. How do I combat the lies telling [him/her] that experimentation is the only way to develop a healthy sexuality? That's exactly what every hormonal teenager wants to hear!

Please direct me to resources that will help me explain the goodness of Your design. Soften my heart and open my ears when [he/she] comes to me with questions, so I can first listen and understand before jumping to a response. Lord, if my child's father is the one being asked the questions, then I pray these words over him as well. Empower me to remain calm when the questions or topics are complex, intimidating, or emotionally charged and—sweet Lord Jesus—help me control the expressions on my face, not exhibiting shock, embarrassment, fear, or any other emotions that might arise. Show me where I need to initiate conversations and when to allow my children to come to me. I pray that I become the safest place for [child's] questions so that [he/she] does not feel the need to ask friends or Dr. Google.

Guide [child] as [he/she] thinks about the kind of person [he/she] would like to marry. Give [him/her] the self-control to reserve sex for marriage as You intended, but also help [him/her] to move beyond the simplistic concept of abstinence and toward a more holistic understanding of healthy and holy sexuality—how it reflects and informs [his/her] entire worldview and even [his/her] perception of You!

Lord, external motivation and the fear of consequences may control a person's behavior, but it doesn't change the heart. I pray that [child] would be *internally* motivated to save sex for marriage out of a desire to honor You, honor [himself/herself], and honor [his/her] future spouse (Romans 1:24), and protect [his/her] future marriage. I pray that You would place godly leaders around [him/her] who will reinforce these concepts so it's not just coming from [his/her] stuffy, old parents. And especially, Lord, give [him/her] friends committed to the same sexual values.

Holy Father, please protect [child's] eyes and mind from pornography so that [his/her] understanding of sex is not tainted with vulgarity, degradation, and violence. Please convict [him/her] when [he/she] is watching television or movies with graphic sexual content. Help [him/her] understand that what is on the screen can warp [his/her] idea of what sex will be like one day. May all [his/her] decisions be in preparation for a healthy and fulfilling sex life in [his/her] future marriage.

Honest IDEA

Once your children reach the age where they or their peers are dating, encourage them to write letters to their future spouses. Every time your children long for connection, they can write another letter. Keep the letters in special boxes for them to give their spouses after marriage. I (Hillary) did this from the time I was 16 on. It helped whenever I found myself longing for marriage, or touch, or connection. I poured it all out to John (though I didn't know his name!) He thought it was pretty cool when I gave it to him after the wedding.

62

Prayer for the Esaus' (the Rough-and-Tumble Boys') Gender Identity

Lord, I lift my son up to You. He's grown from the tiny baby in my arms into a pint-size John the Baptist—a ball of passion who keeps eating bugs. I confess I want to wrap him in duct tape and bolt him to the floor at times. Yet when I am weighed down by the fear he seems to lack, I take comfort in knowing You designed men to be bold—and bold men often start out as foolhardy boys who must be taught to steward their impulses.

So, God, I pray You will help me cultivate his self-control, for a man without it is a wildfire unchecked. Teach me how to shepherd the warrior in my boy and know how to discipline him without crushing his playful spirit or natural curiosity. Give me the wisdom to know when to let him work things out on his own and when to intervene. Lord, bless me with patience to not only put up with, but understand and appreciate his rambunctiousness—without letting him become a little terror! When I feel drowned in the noise, help me channel it to Your glory and not shut it down for the sake of my own comfort. And especially, God, please help him hear Your voice in those moments when hormones or hyperactivity spur him to recklessness.

I pray my son would know that manhood is not just burping contests and bench-pressing. It shows just as much strength to be tender as it does to be tough. Help him see healthy examples of strong Christian men expressing their emotions and know that it's okay for him to have a sensitive heart.

Lord, give me the patience to teach him to use his voice and strength for good, and give him both the wisdom to use his words wisely and the opportunities to use them well. Show him that with his words he can bring great comfort or cause great destruction, for our tongue is like the rudder of a mighty ship, a spark, and a sword (James 3:1-11).

I pray for [son] to feel anchored in his identity as a man, confident that he was created with purpose in Your image. I pray that he would be content as a great leader, or a faithful and devoted follower, so long as he is committed to You. Lord, I recognize that sin has broken our idea of manhood, and this brokenness has fueled hurt and abuse. Yet we know the abuse of Your design is not the design itself. So I place my rough-and-tumble boy in Your hands and surrender my ability to manipulate him to conform to my desires, rather than Your design. I pray for the man he will become—that his boldness becomes boldness for truth, and that the couch he's always standing on will one day be Your Word. I pray he is gentle to the brokenhearted and the weak, but that he would be fierce as a lion when it comes to protecting the little ones being led astray. I pray You will give him wisdom and grace so that he treats others as You have treated us—and no matter what may come, that he will always draw close to You.

Until then, Lord, thank You for Your strength as I nurture this tiny force of nature.

63

Prayer for the Jacobs'
(the Sensitive Boys') Gender Identity

Father God, I am humbled that You blessed me with this sweet boy. I am in awe that masculinity isn't just ninja skills and Nerf battles; it's also beauty, creativity, and gentleness. It's calm talks, paintings on the fridge, and an instinct to nurture those around him. Your design is truly good.

Father, I lift up my gentle-spirited boy. The world is so fickle as it rages against the supposedly toxic "Esau" masculinity, only to belittle the Jacobs as "not man enough." But we know this is a lie from the enemy to mock Your creation. I ask for Your hand of protection as my son grows. I pray that his view of masculinity would be broad enough to include himself as he is—thoughtful, creative, and imaginative. I pray for voices in his life who will celebrate his distinct gifts, praising his unique kind of masculinity without comparing him to other boys. I pray he would view his gifts, personality, and interests as indicators of Your calling for his life, not as deficiencies that need to be overcome or hidden. And I pray for strong relationships with other boys and men who will accept him as he is.

Please teach him to steward his thoughts and his imagination—not disappearing into them as an escape from reality, and not going down rabbit holes that lead him to unhelpful places. I pray for his tendency to obsess over careless critiques; give him the strength to release other people's opinions of him while being sensitive to Your voice and direction in his life.

Lord, give him wisdom as he navigates what's being taught about masculinity by both the world and the church. As the world stretches its definition of manhood to the breaking point, the church can be tempted to narrow it down until it becomes too small to hold every type of man. But Your Word shows many dimensions of masculinity. You chose an emotional shepherd boy who played the harp to lead Israel. You chose the younger brother who loved to cook over the older brother who loved to hunt. And You know my son, who would rather chew glass than participate in a contact sport. This doesn't make him any less of a boy. May Your voice of affirmation be louder than any voice that judges him against stereotypical ideas of masculinity.

You created men to protect, and nurturing is part of that protecting spirit. You gave men the desire to shepherd their family, and that comes, too, from wise counsel. You made men musicians and artists, comforters and caretakers. Men are poets and voices of truth. I am grateful to be a mother to such a boy! Give [son] opportunities to share his gifts for Your glory. Help others to see how You are working through his unique strengths to form his potential to be a world changer for Your glory, but keep the devil from distorting that potential for evil.

I pray, too, that You will challenge him to get out of his comfort zone. Just as boldness needs shepherding, gentleness needs passion. Help him recognize when it is time to be a peacemaker and when it is time to fight. The world will try to take advantage of his calm nature, but I pray You will give him wisdom and courage when those attacks come. I ask that You help me nurture his sense of adventure so that challenges don't feel so daunting.

I pray for his future friendships and family relationships. Help him encounter boys with similar passions so he can find kinship. Bring boys who are more boisterous into his life so he can be challenged and encouraged by rough-and-tumble friends. Open the eyes of family members who might have a one-sided view of manhood; may they also see the man in my boy.

Above all, I pray my boy will hear Your call, then follow the ultimate Artist and loving Father.

64

Prayer for My Daughter's Gender Identity

Lord, I pray for [daughter] as she learns to navigate this world as a girl and later as a woman. God, I hate how hypersexualized our world has become and how it's trying to convince my daughter that her body is a tool to be used for power instead of a temple to be protected and cherished. I pray she would see herself through Your eyes instead of all the filters of social media. I also pray our world's preoccupation with sex would not make her reject the beautiful and womanly parts of herself.

God, may she find herself in the pages of Scripture and discover that womanhood is not a one-size-fits-all mold. Protect her from the pressures of both church and the world, each telling her that she needs to be a certain way in order to be a "real woman." I pray she would be entirely comfortable with how You have made her without trying to impress anyone else or prove a point. I pray she would walk boldly as Your daughter, knowing that boldness does not mean loudness, status, or influence. She can be bold and still be quiet. And she can have a "gentle and quiet spirit" while still speaking her mind (1 Peter 3:4). I pray that You would allow her to discover and walk within her unique personality, embracing her gifts, not judging herself for her weaknesses, and never, ever becoming complacent with her unique sin struggles.

I pray this world's perception of "feminine" would never force her into a box. At the same time, may this world's rejection of traditional femininity never lead her to reject the parts of herself that do fit a stereotype. May she never buy into the lie that masculinity is more important than femininity; may she also know that personality traits and interests aren't gendered. No matter her passions, clothing preferences, personality, or profession, may she never feel like she has to reject her identity as a woman in order to fully "be herself."

I pray for her relationships with other girls, that she would never fall prey to the comparison game or the lie that you have to put someone else down in order to elevate yourself. Help me remind her that intelligence is not a gift to be hidden, nor is it the full measure of a woman. I pray she would be equally comfortable leading the charge as she is playing a supporting role. And please remind me and help me to model the joy of affirming and celebrating others out of the overflow of the love and goodness You shower upon me.

I pray she would reject the world's lie that desiring marriage and motherhood is a lower calling than a career. Protect her from the pressure women face to "do it all." And if marriage or family is not in her future, I pray the church would not make her feel like she is incomplete or missing out on her true calling.

Please, Lord, help me see her as the unique girl that You have created her to be, and help me fan into flame the gifts and talents You have placed within her. I lay before You any expectations of what I think a daughter should be like. She is not mine, Lord; she is Yours. May I see her as You see her.

Section 6

THINGS MY KIDS HAVE TO DEAL WITH

65

Stewarding Popularity Well

Lord, I thank You for gracing my child with being well-liked. Thank You for the favor You have granted [him/her] in the eyes of others. Whatever Your purpose is in this, I pray [he/she] will always recognize that with popularity comes a responsibility to represent You well. Please guard [him/her] from being puffed up or from looking down on others. Help [him/her] handle this mantle with grace and goodness, using [his/her] influence to bring acceptance and community to the outcasts. Help [him/her] show compassion and kindness to those who are not as well-liked as [he/she] is, and to not get jealous of others who are.

Whatever influence You grant [child], may [he/she] use it to bring about good for others and Your kingdom. I pray [he/she] remembers that the grace and favor [he/she] has experienced from others is a gift to be stewarded and not squandered. And if this is just a glorious season that passes from [him/her], may [child] adjust to the change without growing bitter or trying to regain "the glory days." The fear of man leads to all kinds of foolishness. May [he/she] fear You alone, stewarding popularity well without growing addicted to the positive attention. There will be a day when [he/she] needs to stand up for truth in an unpopular way. May [he/she] understand social acceptance to be a temporary gift, not a permanent given.

66

Dealing with Rejection

Lord, rejection cuts right to the very core, telling us we are unworthy and unwanted. I pray that [child] would be able to receive the truth: that You created [him/her] with beautiful and ultimate worth, and that no human opinion can change that. God, I pray that I would be able to hurt with [child] through this rejection, not trying to push [him/her] to process the pain faster than [he/she] can handle. Lord, it is hard to integrate Your words into our hearts in the pain of the moment and the heat of rejection. So please allow [child] to hold on to the truth, even if it's only in word, until [he/she] can tangibly feel the comfort You have provided. Fill [child] with Your peace, Your confidence, Your strength, and Your love.

Lord, we praise You for allowing us to feel rejection, as You, too, were rejected and despised by men (Isaiah 53:3). Please use this painful experience to foster intimacy with [child], and enable [him/her] to flip this rejection on its head—that it would not result in defeat but in empowerment, spurring [child] to speak hope and life into other kids who feel crushed under the weight of rejection. Lord, I pray that [he/she] may be able to show others their value and worth, pointing them to You as their Lord and Savior as well.

Honest HABIT

Every time your children feel rejected or hurt, have them encourage someone else who may feel the same, whether through a compliment, a high five, or an invitation to sit together at lunch. Make every rejection a reminder to turn around and do the opposite for someone else. There are few better ways to break away from self-pity than serving others. It is a balm for a wounded soul.

67

When My Child Feels Alone in Following Christ

Lord, please be near [child] when [he/she] stands alone as the only one of [his/her] peers truly seeking to follow You and live according to Your commands. In [his/her] school, [his/her] job, or even in the youth group—Lord, be [child's] support system when [he/she] feels alone.

When rejected, remind [him/her] that the world hated You first (John 15:18). I pray You will take [his/her] shame and one day replace it with praise and renown (Zephaniah 3:19). Comfort [child] when [he/she] is fearful of retribution for being faithful to Your Word, and give [him/her] courage to endure any consequences for standing firm in Your truth. Give [child] a healthy self-respect that allows [him/her] to act upon [his/her] convictions while exercising Your kindness that leads to repentance (Romans 2:4).

Protect [child's] heart and mind from lies of the enemy, especially if the enemy tries to convince [him/her] that living for You is not worth the cost. May [he/she] count it all joy that the testing of [his/her] faith is worth the spiritual maturity as You make [him/her] perfect and complete (James 1:2-4). And as [child] develops a wholehearted devotion to You, may it never come at the expense of loving like Jesus loved. As [he/she] walks according to Your commands, may [he/she] be the hands and feet of Jesus to those who reject [him/her], developing a healthy humility and not succumbing to self-righteous comparison.

Honest CONVERSATION

My (Hillary's) pastor used to have a saying: "You're not always being persecuted for being righteous. Sometimes you're being persecuted for being obnoxious." Talk to your kids about what this might mean, and encourage them to evaluate their own attitudes as they live out their faith. Make sure that, in their zeal to live for Christ, they are not growing puffed up with self-righteousness (even though this is a very easy coping mechanism for feeling alone in the faith). It is easy to develop a persecution complex that prevents us from seeing when our commitment to truth has made us become cold and loveless.

68

Good Friends for My Son

God, I pray for good friends for my son. I pray You would provide him with other boys who share his interests and have a desire to pursue You. I pray for laughter and fun and plenty of scraped knees to go around. But I also pray for at least one of his friends in the group to be aware enough to speak up before they do something truly stupid and dangerous. When there is temptation to impress other boys (or, heaven forbid, to impress girls), I pray they would exercise wisdom, discretion, and the common sense that is all too uncommon among a group of boys all trying to outdo each other.

I pray against the temptation that boredom can bring. When trouble goes looking for them, may they be willing to turn the other way. I pray You would form in them a sense of godly bravery and independence. At the same time, when they are tempted to see how close to the fire they can get without being burned, I ask that Lady Wisdom would intervene before too much damage is done (Proverbs 8).

I pray for friends who will stand against a culture that tells them manhood is earned by using and disrespecting women. I pray that my son and his friends would be godly influences among the other boys at school, standing as brave warriors who will protect every girl in their community—no matter if she is a love interest or not. I pray that they would vehemently stand against any dishonor or shame that is directed at young women by classmates who demand inappropriate pictures or revel in making girls the objects of inappropriate stories.

Grant my son friends who are ambitious enough to move beyond video games and into activities that cultivate their minds and bodies. I pray for emotional safety among them, so they are willing to say the hard things to each other when one of them steps out of line. Above all, may they spur one another on toward godliness and good deeds, and may these boys grow into men of honor (Hebrews 10:24).

69

Good Friends for My Daughter

Dear God, You created friendship, and when it blossoms, it's beautiful. It was not good for Adam to be alone, so You gave him Eve (Genesis 2:18). And since the day of that first friendship, we as humans have enjoyed deep friendships with one another. Friendship is so good, Lord! But it's not always easy to find or make friends. My heart aches for [daughter] to find deep, lasting friendships—or at the very least, good friends for the season she's in.

I pray You would help my daughter to make friends. Please, God, give her the kind of friend who will text her to meet at the park or just to chat, a friend who will share a lunch when she forgets hers, or a friend who will wait for her on the swings. She needs a friend with whom she can share her secrets, and someone to turn to for advice on a tricky situation. Give [daughter] friends who not only have kindness and humor, but also discernment and conviction. Lord, please give her these kinds of friends, and help her to become a good friend too; lead her to become a friend who is kind, gentle, loyal, and wise. And as these friends grow up and face more challenges, may these relationships serve to sharpen each girl. May they point each other toward Christ and away from the ways of the world. If they compete, let it be for who can love others the most, with both truth and grace.

Lord, I pray for a friend who has [daughter's] back when other girls seek to tear her down. Please make them brave together as they stand against peer pressure and the temptation to compromise. I pray that the security they find in each other will protect them from trying to get unhealthy attention from boys; may they hold one another to a higher standard than this culture demands. I pray they would say hard things to each other, pray together, study together, and praise You together.

I pray for bonds that will last a lifetime. And even if she cannot yet build this kind of epic, lifelong friendship, please allow my daughter to have just enough good-hearted friends this year to not feel lonely. Thank You, Lord, for friendship, and for hearing my prayer.

70

Sports Participation

Lord, as [child] enters the world of sports, I pray that this will be a positive experience. Help the coach to bring out the best in [him/her], to nurture [child's] talents, instruct with patience, discipline with kindness, communicate well, and bring no harm of any kind. Help [child] to have a teachable spirit and a willingness to try hard. May [he/she] strive and do [his/her] best, to accept [his/her] limitations and to stretch [his/her] potential.

I pray that [child] will be an example of excellent sportsmanship and an encouraging and selfless teammate. May [he/she] rejoice with those who succeed and weep with those who fall short. If [he/she] has setbacks, let [him/her] learn well and come back stronger. Use sports to teach [child] godly principles of self-control, discipline, and compassion.

Help our family balance the time and emphasis we place on sports. If sports or other hobbies are becoming an idol—crowding out leisure, family, or proper devotion to God—may I have the fortitude to straighten out our priorities, pruning unnecessary activities until there is once again time for rest, discipleship, and family bonding.

71

Moving

Moving is exciting and hard at the same time, Lord, and I'm concerned about how it will affect my children. Especially leaving behind friends, cherished routines, traditions, beloved teachers, and trusted physicians. Who am I kidding? *I'm* worried about all this for me as well! Please help us move through this transition gracefully. Let us pack up the good memories to carry with us while unpacking the grief over what is being lost.

You are the God of hope. You never leave us. You never forsake us. You are just as much with us in our new home/city/neighborhood/school as You were before. Help us to embrace this new adventure. In Your timing, bring us friends and everything else we need to flourish in our new surroundings. Use these chapters of life to continue writing our family's story as we seek to follow You wherever You take us.

Honest IDEA

If you are moving far enough away that your kids won't see their friends anymore, put together letters or videos from all their friends so your children can have reminders of the many people who love them. As you settle into the new place, help your children compile photo albums to look back on when they are lonely.

72

Welcoming a New Pet

Lord, we are welcoming a new pet into our home. Guide us as we experience all the joys and the irritations of the adjustment. Use [pet] to teach my children how to care for Your creation, how to develop responsibility, and how to wisely exercise dominion over the creatures You have given to us as humans. You say in Your Word that the righteous man has regard for the life of his beast (Proverbs 12:10). Help my children to learn to lead by serving, providing, and taking care of this animal that is under their care. We thank You in advance for the sloppy kisses, purrs, playtime, walks, poop scooping, slithering, squawking, and any other delightful songs brought into our home by this furry, scaly, or feathery friend.

73

Saying Goodbye to a Beloved Pet

Lord, we are heartbroken at the death of our dear [pet]. We thank You for the joy that [pet] brought us. As we grieve this loss, bring to our memory all the fun and sweet times so our tears may be mingled with smiles. Help us remember that death was not part of Your original plan, so our grief is natural and expected. May this loss make us long even more for our eternal home with You, where the sting of death can no longer reach us. We humans were not created for mortality but for eternity. But while here on this earth, Lord, teach us how to weather the cycles of life with hope. Comfort us as we experience the painful parts of living in a fallen world. We again thank You for the time You gave us with [pet]. Please fill our hearts with joy once again.

Nightmares

Oh Lord, my poor [child] keeps having disturbing nightmares. They disturb me, too, and my sleep. You are all-knowing, so You know the cause—is it just a childhood thing that will pass? Has [child] seen, heard, or experienced something to set this off? Is there something deeper and darker? You are the light, Lord; nothing is hidden from You, so I am asking You to bring the source of these bad dreams to light. If [child] is filling [his/her] mind with dark images, may these dreams serve to remind [him/her] how important it is to guard our eyes.

As [his/her] mom, give me compassion to help [child] through this tough night. In Your great mercy, I call on You to restore sweet slumber to my child. Show [child] that [his/her] nightmares are not real, but Your comfort is; Your Word is the lullaby to our souls, because "greater is He who is in you than he who is in the world" (1 John 4:4 NASB). May we both be able to lie down and sleep in peace, oh Lord, for You make us dwell in safety (Psalm 4:8).

Dating

Oh God, here we go. How did we get here so fast? Honestly, I have dreaded this moment because I know all the things that can go wrong—the hurt, the temptation, the danger, and the pressure. I pray that [child] would discover what [he/she] needs and wants in a future spouse without picking up baggage from dating that will make [his/her] marriage more difficult. I pray [he/she] and whomever [he/she] dates would get to know one another without placing themselves in positions that will tempt them to behave like husband and wife rather than boyfriend and girlfriend; give them wisdom to set healthy, godly boundaries and the internal motivation to stick to them.

May [child] treat each significant other in the way [he/she] hopes [his/her] future spouse is being treated. For every relationship that does not end in marriage, I pray that the two would be able to part on friendly terms, both able to say without hesitation that they prepared the other to be an even better husband or wife for someone else, and also able to speak well of each other.

Keep [his/her] father and me attuned to any red flags or danger signs as [child] navigates this new realm. Heaven forbid that [he/she] be harmed in any way in this relationship, but if so, show me how to handle it in a way that still honors You while advocating for [child]. Be the mender of [his/her] heart if or when it is broken. Protect [his/her] ability to trust others in the future, knowing that if nothing else, [he/she] will always be able to trust You. God, I wish we could just fast-forward to marriage, but I know that's not how this works. I pray that any negativity I might have from past bad dating experiences would not hinder my ability to help [child] navigate the world of dating.

Teenagers with Raging Hormones

Father, please help me love my crazy teenagers. Help me to endure every sarcastic remark and angry rebuttal uttered in a hormonal haze. Help me love them through every eye roll, grunt, and exasperated sigh. Remind them they really do want to learn about their changing bodies from their father and me and not from the world. Even when they act embarrassed of our love, remind me that they secretly appreciate the tenderness and care.

For my daughter, I pray over the indignity of acne, the insecurity of bodily development, and the discomfort of periods. Please protect our relationship—I remember the endless friction between me and my own mother, and I do not want this for us. Help me to teach my daughter to honor You with her actions and speech even when she feels completely off-kilter, even when she feels as though her body is rebelling against her. May our home not be ruled by her constantly changing emotions. Help me to be empathetic to her struggles without enabling an improper response. May she come to understand the blessing of womanhood, even when it seems like it is all cost and no benefit. May she also respect and honor the young men in her life during this awkward time. Help me teach her to not belittle or ridicule them as they are learning how to become men.

For my son, I pray over his cracking voice and his awkwardly growing body. I pray against the war going on in his mind as he seeks to honor You and the women around him. I pray for patience when it seems as though all his brain cells have migrated to his biceps. Help me remember that this stage will eventually pass, and in place of my bright boy will be a bright young man. Also help me to teach my son how to respect and honor the young females in his life during this time, making sure he is aware of how casual teasing with them can cut far deeper than it does with his guy friends.

Lord, be with my kids' father and me as we navigate this new stage of development. Remind us what it felt like at that age so we can be gracious yet firm for the good of our teenagers' spiritual development. This situation is not unique to us or to our children. You created their bodies and hearts to endure these changes. Please help us to coexist peacefully together. Though our home is hormonal, may it still be a happy one.

Forgotten Items

My child has forgotten something again, Lord. Do I come to the rescue or not? Grant me wisdom in how to proceed. If this is an opportunity to show Your grace, may I joyfully rearrange my schedule. Help my child recognize the mercy I grant [him/her] as a reflection of You, and enable [him/her] to extend it to others who need it because [he/she] has received it [himself/herself].

If this behavior is part of a larger pattern, give me the self-control to not swoop in so [child] will learn from the consequences of this mistake and be less likely to repeat it. Where favor is needed from a teacher, coach, or friend, please grant it. Take this situation and use it for [child's] growth. I want to hold [him/her] to a high standard, but may I not expect more from [child] than [he/she] is capable of.

78

Pressure to Fit In

Lord, [child] is being pressured on all sides: by me, by friends, by the world. Some amount of pressure can be good, but too much can cause someone to break.

As [child] tries to decide who [he/she] is, I pray [he/she] will never lose a grip on the biblical values we have tried to instill in [him/her]. As [he/she] asks, "Who will I follow—the Lord or the world?" help [him/her] remember that Jesus Himself is the Way. There is no better guide for walking in the truth, so give [him/her] the heart and courage to take the narrow path that leads to righteousness, even if it takes away popularity points or makes [him/her] feel alone. Help [him/her] not be afraid to travel Your path alone until You provide friends to travel alongside [him/her].

May [child] embrace the adventure of following You in a culture that doesn't. Give [him/her] the necessary survival skills. When [he/she] is asked, "Why don't you [fill in the blank with whatever debauchery is being encouraged by peers]?" help [him/her] to speak with spiritual conviction unburdened by the condemnation of others. Use [his/her] strength under pressure to inspire [his/her] friends to desire You for themselves. When the pressure feels like too much for [child] to bear, let our home be a release valve and let me be [his/her] refuge, encouraging [him/her] to use this pressure to become more like You and less like the world.

Honest REMINDER

Although it's hard to be a Christian in this society, rejoice that the real Christians are being revealed! People aren't just claiming to be Christians because it's cool. It's not cool anymore. Kids love to see themselves as rebels. Remind them that, in a world such as ours, following Christ can be the most radical thing they can do.

79

Protection Against Comparison

Lord, help me set reasonable expectations for myself and my children. When it comes to grades, sports, performance, friends, other moms, and other families, keep our eyes on You instead of on the standards set by others. Help us remember that our self-image is built on being made in the *imago dei*—image of God—not the *imago me*. Instruct me to know when average is okay. When failure happens—my own or my kids'—grant us humility to learn, improve, move on, and not be defined by it but rather *refined* through it. The jealousy monster is real. Let it not cause havoc in our house; may we slay it with the sword of Your Spirit, which is the Word of God.

80

Broken Hearts

God, [child] is hurting so badly right now. I have the luxury of perspective, and it can be easy for me to downplay the real pain [he/she] is going through. I pray that I would not minimize [his/her] heartache, but would be a safe place for [him/her] to be vulnerable, to grieve, and to process these emotions.

When my presence is unwelcome, I pray You would meet my child in [his/her] sorrow, reminding [him/her] that there is no earthly pain You did not experience first. You were mocked. You were betrayed. You were rejected by Your best friends. Oh Lord, You say in Psalm 34:18 that You are close to the brokenhearted and save those who are crushed in spirit. Remind [child] of this promise.

God, it is sometimes hard to predict when little hurts will become life-shaping trauma. I pray that [child] would feel this pain without being consumed by it. Help me give [him/her] the space to heal without giving [him/her] so much space that the pain spirals out of control. Alert me if this behavior is pointing toward other wounds, and give me the wisdom to know when to engage and when to back away. Oh God, [child] is Your child first and foremost. Please be with [him/her] while [his/her] heart is breaking.

Section 7

WELCOME TO THE RUMBLLLLLLE

When I Have Been Wronged (and Want to Release the Kraken)

Lord, I have been wronged and I am angry. I feel like James and John, the sons of thunder; I just want You to bring the fire of heaven down and destroy those who hurt me (Luke 9:54). But I thank You, Lord, that I can bring my anger to You. I can bring my pain, my hurt, my desire for revenge and lay it at Your feet. David didn't feel the need to censor himself in the Psalms, so neither will I.

Lord, please calm my heart as my brain plays the scene over and over again in my head, reminding me of just how right I was and how wrong [person] was. I know that this kind of obsessing will not lead to Your righteousness. And things are rarely black-and-white. Please reveal to me how I have contributed to the situation. Even if I'm 99 percent right, I should still own the 1 percent where I'm wrong. But let's be honest…I'm probably not 99 percent guiltless.

Oh God, I can't go back and change what happened. Remind me of the times when I have failed, when I have been the one who has brought hurt. If I'm honest with myself, there is nothing that [person] has done to me that I haven't done to You first, my Savior and my God. Seventy, times seven, times infinity, God, You have forgiven me. Who am I to withhold Your forgiveness from another?

Lord, I pray against this spirit of revenge that I feel screaming in my ear, coaxing me into all the things I should do to protect my reputation. Guard me from the lies of the enemy, which feed off my indignation. Show me how to proceed in this situation and how to wisely express my anger and hurt in a way that might lead to reconciliation. And if returning to this relationship is unwise, Lord, please give me the strength to release [person] to You, knowing there is only so much I can do to establish peace. For my own sake, help me replace my anger with Your compassion. Or at least help me to release into Your hands what was done to me.

God, forgiveness doesn't mean that what was done is suddenly okay. Forgiveness is exempting myself from being judge and jury. And though I want to tell the world what was done to me, set a guard over my mouth. God, give me Your power to take the high road, even when I want so badly to grab justice for myself. You say in Your Word that vengeance is Yours to repay (Deuteronomy 32:35). Bring to light what needs to be brought to light. Give me the patience to right the wrongs that were done to me in Your time, in Your way.

Honest IDEA

It is really easy to obsess over a situation when you feel you were wronged. For me (Hillary), rumination occurs when my brain wants to make sure it remembers everything that happened accurately. To stop my obsessive thoughts, I have started putting everything into a Word document so my brain can say, *Phew! It's documented somewhere. I don't have to keep thinking about it.* I can add to it as I remember things. But I don't show this document to anyone. It is solely for the purpose of making my brain stop obsessing. This advice may help some people release the event and stop fixating on remembering the details. For others, it might make you obsess more. Know thyself, Mama Bear. If it makes you obsess more, (and prevents you from releasing the situation) then disregard this idea.

Before Engaging in Conflict Resolution

Lord, my heart is in my stomach as I approach this conflict zone. I pray for humility to see my own flaws, grace to see where others are hurting, patience to navigate defense mechanisms, and strength to absorb whatever anger is sent in my direction. Lord, make me an instrument of Your peace, remembering that the path to peace is sometimes painful. Sweeping things under the rug may work in the short run, but it does not lead to resolution. Give me the courage to bring unpleasant things into the open. May we work toward *actual* peace, not just the appearance of it. Help me release any blame unfairly placed on my shoulders and own any that is mine to own. Help me to repent without making excuses, and to grant mercy as I would want mercy granted to me. Above all, help me to see [person] through Your eyes of love as a fellow broken vessel still in the process of conforming to Your image.

83

Loving the Unlovable

Lord, I did not treat [person] the way I should have. Thank You, Lord, for Your conviction; please continue moving in my heart. I recognize how many times I've been unlovable, difficult, and socially awkward. You have loved me anyway. Lord, thank You for never giving up on me. Please give me the grace that I should have shown [person]. You say in the Sermon on the Mount, "Blessed are the merciful, for they will be shown mercy" (Matthew 5:7). Lord, I need mercy so often. I lose my temper. I make a fool of myself. I represent You poorly. And dare I even admit it? I can be downright *annoying*, which sometimes feels like the worst social sin of all.

Lord, make me an instrument of Your love and mercy and unconditional acceptance. I pray You would bring it to my attention when others overlook my flaws and oddities, so I in turn can have a ready picture of what I am when others have flaws and oddities that are annoying to me. Lord, thank You for never giving up on me. Please help me take responsibility for the unloving way in which I treated [person], apologize sincerely, and do anything else that is needed to make amends. And tomorrow, give me a special helping of grace for [person], so I can love [him/her] with the compassion and acceptance You have showered upon me.

When Everyone
Is at Each Other's Throat

Lord, we stop right this moment to remember that we are not each other's enemies; we are on the same team.

God, we resist whatever spirits of confusion, anger, or miscommunication are trying to steal our joy. Once again we confess to being short-tempered, entitled, or quarrelsome. We humbly ask that You reveal to us individually where we have been wrong, and we pray You will guide us as we seek to heal whatever wounds were just created. I pray You would open our eyes to any pain the other is experiencing, so we might see each other with Your grace and compassion.

May Your spirit of peace enter this house and silence the voice of the accuser. We ask that clear communication and love be present in all our conversations. Lord, hem us in, "behind and before" (Psalm 139:5). Protect this home from anything that is causing strife and division.

85

When Husband and Daddy Duties Compete...and I Need My Husband

I love my husband, Lord, but I feel like I rarely see him, especially without the kids around. My heart is heavy, Father, and I confess that I'm struggling to share him. He works so hard, he gets home, and then the kids want to bask in his attention. I'm so grateful for the wonderful family You've given me, and I know the kids need their father—but I need my husband too. I'm starting to resent feeling like his last priority, and our marriage is suffering because of it.

I miss my husband. I miss date nights. I miss having long, heart-to-heart conversations that *aren't* about kids. Father, remind us that before we were Mom and Dad, we were husband and wife. (And before that, we were boyfriend and girlfriend!) Show us how to prioritize each other without taking attention away from the kids. Father God, protect our marriage. Help me to have the courage to talk to my husband about how I feel, but without making him feel guilty for my needs. Show me where I can serve him as a wife; help me encourage him and fill his sails so he has the extra energy.

Help me to love my family sacrificially while also finding the courage to speak up about my longings. Turn my heart toward my husband and his toward mine, and help us both to draw closer to You. Help me speak to him with love and humility as we work together to glorify You in how we raise our family. Thank You so much for giving me a man who loves being both a husband and father. Thank You for our close-knit family. Help me to never lose sight of what a blessed woman I am!

(Review the Honest Step on the next page.)

Make sure you and your husband are getting intentional alone time. If a babysitter isn't financially feasible, find another couple whom you can trade babysitting nights with so that each couple has a date night from time to time.

86

Parenting the Children I Have (and Releasing Who I Think They Should Be)

Oh Lord, I couldn't wait to become a mom. I'll admit, I've romanticized motherhood and created an idealized version of the child I expected to have. I imagined [his/her] life and future in ways that pleased my human heart. I pictured the sports [he/she] would play, the interests we'd share, the matching clothes we'd wear. But real life has shown me how my idealized vision of [child] is preventing me from loving the child I have. I confess that I often struggle to understand [him/her]. I am trying to parent [him/her] the way [he/she] needs to be parented, but I don't even know what [he/she] needs half the time—and when I try something that would have worked with me, it backfires. Sometimes, I just don't understand [him/her], and I know [he/she] doesn't understand me.

God, I pray You would open my eyes to areas where I am projecting my own expectations onto [child]. Please reveal to me the unique way You have made [him/her], that I may cultivate [his/her] strengths without fixating on [his/her] weaknesses. Help me to support [him/her] in the interests *You* have given [him/her], no matter how little they interest me. Lord, I don't want to stand in the way of [him/her] fulfilling *Your* plans for [him/her]. [Child] is Your child first.

Grant me a kingdom mindset and eternal vision for the child you have given me. Give me the courage to help mold [child] into *Your* image instead of trying to conform [him/her] to mine. As I mother [him/her], empower me to disciple [him/her] well according to the way You made [him/her].

Calming Down Before Disciplining My Child

Lord, I am about to blow it—please hold me back! I feel so mad I could scream. I need You to calm me down. I need a time-out before I can lovingly dispense discipline, because right now it would not be coming out of love. Lord, remind me of the times when You have been patient with me after I've strayed or disobeyed. Remind me of my own rebellion and failings as I seek to wisely discipline my child. Let my motives be to restore and instruct [him/her], not to belittle [him/her]. Give me wisdom to make the punishment fit the crime, no more and no less.

God, You alone know what [child] needs to learn from this lesson. I release my anger to You. I thank You for the times when You have redirected me. I know full well that discipline is never fun, but it produces a fruit of righteousness and peace for those who allow it (Hebrews 12:11). Lord, calm my heart. Wipe away my own tears. Give me compassion for [child] as You have shown me compassion time and time again. I pray that everything I do would be for my child's loving correction, and that [he/she] would not only gain the skills to become a successful adult, but also become one who loves and fears Your commands.

Asking for My Child's Forgiveness

Heavenly Father, I have blown it. More times than I care to mention, but especially right now. Today, I need to ask my child for forgiveness. Seeing myself more clearly has shown me how easily my sin can leave lasting scars on this little person You've given me to raise. Oh Lord, please protect my child's heart and mind from me when I fail to live as a loving example of Christ.

I thank Your Holy Spirit for pricking my pride and bursting my bubble of self-righteousness. I want to be a superhero mom, never making mistakes or messing up my witness in front of my kids. Yet here we are. I'm not a superhero. Today, I was the villain. As much as it humbles me to admit my error, isn't that Your point? I need to demonstrate humility that leads to repentance, and then form the words and get them out of my dry mouth.

Help me make my apology true—not sugarcoated, not euphemistic, and especially not in the form of an excuse. Help me to name exactly what I did wrong and why I need to ask for forgiveness. Lord, my children will learn how to repent and apologize based on how their father and I model these things. Use this apology as a demonstration that gives them the courage and permission to do the same whenever they have wronged another. Use it for my sanctification and for theirs.

Grant me patience if they are not able to forgive me right away. Help me release my disappointment in myself, knowing I have done what I can do to seek reconciliation. Please restore our relationship. And if my child has not yet accepted Your forgiveness for [his/her] sins, use this exchange to move [him/her] ever closer to You.

When I Really Don't Like Someone but Want To

Lord, I don't know if I can—or should—admit this out loud, so let's keep this between us: I am really struggling to like [person].

God, I thank You for the gift of relationships. I thank You for the value they serve in refining us and challenging us to live in community despite personality differences. I *want* to like [person]. I do. I know I cannot control anything but my own response, so I bring this to Your feet.

Lord, I pray for the ability to see [person] through Your eyes. I pray the things that bug me will just not bug me anymore—or at least will bug me less! You made [person]. You know [his/her] history, quirks, trauma, and triumphs. I know that when You think of [person], You can see a masterpiece where I just see a hot mess. I just don't see [person] the way You do, but I want to.

Remind me to speak encouragement when I see [person] doing whatever [he/she] does well. In the areas where we have personality differences, reveal to me the benefits of being like [person]. Where there is pain and [person] is acting out of fear or instinct, give me the words and actions to be a safe place. Where I feel misunderstood, please give me the ability to communicate.

Lord, You say that as far as it depends on us, we are to live at peace with all people (Romans 12:18). So as far as it depends on me in this relationship, may I do and say the things that foster kindness, friendship, and closeness. Where things are outside of my control, I pray for the ability to release and to absorb—as You absorbed on our behalf.

90

Establishing Boundaries with Toxic Family Members

Lord, You are the author of creation, so You alone know how much sin has warped us. Oh God, I cannot subject my family to [person] anymore. It is no longer about peace but about protecting those whom You have put in my care. God, I pray for the wisdom to know when and where to set healthy boundaries. Instill in me a supernatural love for [person] that can only come from You. Lord, I've done everything I can possibly do to live with [person] in a peaceful relationship, but it is no longer healthy.

Self-righteousness is crouching at my door, hoping to woo me with all the ways that I am right and [person] is wrong—but I crucify any sense of self-righteousness before You. Separation from others is never Your first plan. At the same time, [person] is family, and I cannot just cease all relationship. I need Your wisdom to place firm and healthy boundaries for the good of our family, God. I pray for our hearts as we heal from this broken relationship. I pray You would give us eyes to see where You are working in [person's] life, and may we also celebrate each victory together. But where there is recalcitrance and hardness, God, may our hearts not become wounded and calloused.

Lord, living at peace with everyone does not always mean subjecting ourselves to their presence. We can live at peace from a distance, knowing You are the restorer of all things. God, please work in [person's] heart, showing [him/her] how [his/her] actions are pushing people away. I know [he/she] does not want to be alone, and I know that a person would never act in the way [person] does unless they were in a lot of pain. So, Lord, bring healing to the parts of [him/her] that need it. I pray that I would communicate our family's need to separate in a way that is unemotional and leaves the door open for future relationship should [person's] behavior change.

God, I know it is only by Your grace that I have not found myself in the same situation as [person]. Please search my heart for the areas where I have wounded others. May I never be at rest with my own sin. Thank You for bringing all things to light and restoring all things in eternity.

Honest REMINDER

We can care so much about unity and love that we forget that healthy boundaries can be loving as well, especially for those in our family who need protection.

91

Prayer for My Husband's Ex-Wife

Lord, I pray for my husband's ex-wife. If there is any conflict in their relationship, I pray they would be willing to put that aside for the good of their children. Give them grace for one another. Please bring her enough comfort and peace to not be threatened by me as her children's stepmom. I ask that our interactions at sports and school events will be friendly. Give me patience to co-parent with her in love. Let us both always put the children's needs above our own desires. When I do not understand her actions, help me give her the benefit of the doubt. Help me not jump to conclusions about her thoughts toward me. If I hear hurtful things she has said about me and my biological children, please soften my heart. Help me be at peace and accept that her opinion of me and my children has nothing to do with our worth.

I ask that You would bless her and fill her home with joy. Be present in her home. Put a longing to know You deep in her heart. I pray she raises our children knowing the gospel. When she struggles with parenting, work, or marriage, lead her to You for guidance. Bless her finances. Help me not judge or scrutinize her spending. Show me her children—my stepchildren—through Your eyes if I ever feel offended or insecure. Put in my heart a love and understanding for them that is stronger than my hurt and fears. When I have doubts, remind me You are a mighty God in control of this situation. Lord, thank You for Your unconditional love. Thank You for teaching us to love one another. Help me love my husband's ex-wife.

Section 8

DOES THIS PRAYER MAKE ME LOOK FAT?

92

When I Just
Want to Pee Alone

Dear God, I'm so grateful for my children. Truly, I am. I longed for and prayed for them, but some days I just want to pee alone. I miss my life before them. I miss *me* before them. I miss sleeping peacefully, cooking whatever I wanted, leaving the house whenever I wanted, and going wherever I wanted. Is that too much to wish for? Good grief, nothing humbles you like motherhood.

Thank You, God, for the reminder that it's not all about me. Help me to remember how sacred this calling is. Help me to cherish my children and serve them sacrificially without expecting appreciation or reciprocation. Help me remember that this is a special season. Before long I will have "me" back, and then I will miss these days. Help me to remain grateful, patient, and loving. But in the meantime, I feel like I could really regroup if I could, just this once, pee without an audience.

93

When Social Media Has Warped My View of Motherhood

Lord, I love social media. Motherhood can be so isolating, and sometimes the virtual community can feel like the only community I have. Thank You for the blessings that social media can bring, but I pray You would help me realize when I'm using it because I have a desire to escape instead of a desire to connect.

I confess, Lord, that I often interact more with people online than I do the people in my own church. This isn't healthy; it prevents me from seeking in-person fellowship. I fixate on an edited version of myself and others instead of focusing on real life, which is happening right in front of me. Most of all, it feeds me lies about what motherhood should look like.

Please forgive me for the times I've allowed pictures to shape my parenting more than Your Word. I judge myself for not taking the vacations, making the crafts, or creating the experiences that other mothers provide. I curate my profile trying to deceive others into thinking my family has the picture-perfect life; meanwhile, I participate in other moms' likewise deception toward me. We fight and inwardly compete over who has crafted the best façade, holding ourselves to a standard that we all know isn't real. Why do we do this to ourselves? Oh God, why am I allowing it to continue?

Human approval, praise, likes, and comments have fueled this addiction, and I repent of making my vanity a higher priority than authenticity, humility, and the discipleship of my child. In my desire to be perfect in ways that don't matter, I've missed opportunities to demonstrate Your love and grace in ways that do. Give me the strength to break off any addictions to social media that are fueling the problem. Change my desires. Change my values. May I fear losing out on Your refining fire more than I fear losing out on meaningless online engagement.

94

When My Mouth
Gets Me in Trouble

Oh Lord, You say in Your Word that the tongue is the hardest member of the body to control. I did not honor You in my speech today. I pray for the humility to apologize to those I have hurt. I cannot say I didn't mean what I said, because Your Word says that out of the heart, the mouth speaks (Matthew 12:34). So, Lord, I pray You would reveal to me what my mind has been meditating on that would cause such ugliness to come forth. Whatever it is, please give me the strength and the self-discipline to remove its toxic influence and replace it with things that are true, wholesome, pure, lovely, admirable, and praiseworthy (Philippians 4:8).

95

When I'm Tempted to Use a
Prayer Request as Gossip

It's tempting, Lord, to share information I know about another in the form of a prayer request—but is my sharing truly coming from a desire to help my friend? Or is it a back door to gossip? Check my motives, Lord. Would I want someone to do this to me? Is this exchange necessary, or is the information better kept to myself? Do I need my friend's permission to share? Am I betraying trust rather than trusting You? Help me be brutally honest with myself and with You. Open my heart to obedience, and shut my mouth to gossip.

When I Want to Paint the Picture Prettier Than It Is

Lord, I know I can confide in You. You already know everything, and I couldn't hide from You even if I wanted to. When it comes to those around me, though, I'm a little less candid.

Lipstick on a pig, false eyelashes on a toad. Whatever You want to call it, Lord, I am not being honest with the people around me when I share a dressed-up version of my messy life. My social media makes me look like I'm thriving, but I am trying to disguise reality. I say I am doing fine, when I should really admit I'm falling apart. I say the family is great, when in reality, we could use prayer. But how can we help each other in our deepest needs if we never get below a surface level in our conversations? If I admit that I don't have it all together, could I be the catalyst to inspire others to open up as well?

Lord, You desire truth in the innermost parts, so make us a community of authenticity. That may mean spilling our guts so we can spit out the yuck. Please start bringing together trustworthy people who desire to know and be known. I pray You would cultivate a community of confidantes and prayer warriors to lift one another up. I pray against any judgmental spirits that have held us captive to comfortable lies rather than expose uncomfortable truths. We cannot walk this journey alone, and we cannot truly walk together unless we are honest about where we are.

Honest HABIT

Call (or get together with) one friend and confess how you often don't show the real you. Ask her if she could use prayer in an area where she is struggling. Commit to being "more real" and praying together regularly.

Unhealthy Fixations

Lord, I confess that [thing I am obsessing over] is starting to have too much mastery over my life. It's what I think about. I plan around it. It determines if I feel happy or sad, peaceful, or stressed. It determines if my day is good or bad. Lord, *nothing* should have that kind of power over me. I'll call it what it is: an idol. Forgive me for bowing my heart to another. [Thing] is not easy to give up. I ask You to kill my desire for it. But at the same time, Lord, I know that living in this fallen world means that temptation will never fully die. It just keeps crawling back, wheezing, weak, but ready to be renewed.

You have called me to die to myself and to live for You. You have called me to repent and to turn from my sins. I pray that You would help me in this journey of taking up my cross to follow You. My character is not grown by You making things easier but by You strengthening me to make hard decisions on a daily basis. And yet I also confess my fear. I'm scared to let go of this. *What if life is as miserable without it as I imagine?* No. I refuse to be mastered by anyone but You, my Lord and my God; I will not be enslaved to anything but righteousness (Romans 6:15-23). Strengthen my resolve. Please help me to get out from underneath the power that [thing] has over me.

Honest EVALUATION

Identifying that something is mastering you is the first step to breaking free. Ask the Lord to reveal one thing that is totally unnecessary yet has a hold over your mind and your schedule. Then, test yourself to release it for a full two weeks. (Can't leave the house without makeup? Go without for two full weeks. Browsing social media? Go silent for two weeks.)

Prayer over Habitual Sin

Lord, I've done it again. I keep returning to [habitual sin], only to hate myself for it. Or I at least pretend to, because that's the only way I can justify falling in the same way over and over. Lord, the things I know I *shouldn't* do are the things I keep doing. And the things that I know I *should* do I struggle to do (Romans 7:15-24). Oh God, please rescue me from my flesh, which wages war against my soul (1 Peter 2:11).

Lord, I hear stories of others and their total transformation. I know I can't force change to happen within myself. Something keeps drawing me to [habitual sin], lying to me, telling me that [sin] is more satisfying than You. God, I won't ever stop the fight between myself and [habitual sin] but I will change my prayer:

Oh God, help me to see Your beauty, Your glory, and Your majesty. Overwhelm me with Your holiness and Your love and Your righteousness. God, I beg You to reveal Yourself to my heart and my mind in a way that completely transforms my affections. I cannot manage this by sheer willpower. I must be drawn to something else even more. Oh my God, draw me to You more than I'm drawn to [habitual sin]. Heal my broken heart that is so desperately trying to meet its own legitimate needs in an illegitimate way.

99

When I'm Too Comfortable with a Shallow Faith

Lord, try as I might to have this relationship with You, I *still* find myself knowing more about You than knowing You personally. It's like being in a fan club: all the facts and none of the closeness. God, I don't feel like I have that intimacy that comes from truly knowing You. Sometimes I have the right head knowledge. Other times I'm complacent with worshipping a version of You that may or may not correspond to the God of Scripture. Or I substitute actual Bible study and instead pick and choose my favorite happy verses that tell me things I already want to hear, ignoring the parts of Scripture that make me uncomfortable.

I want to know You, all of You, even the parts that are difficult to understand. Right now, I picture myself meeting You face-to-face one day, and the interaction includes a stiff handshake with a "nice to finally meet You in person." I don't want it to be like that. I want it to be like meeting a cherished friend to whom I've spent a lifetime pouring out my heart. I want to run to Your arms, confident that I knew the real You while I was here on earth. Lord, please make my walk with You more personal. May my knowledge *of* You and my relationship *with* You never outpace each other.

Lord, I don't care what You have to do to show me who You are. And yes, I realize this is a dangerous prayer to pray. When I am truly abiding in You, the cares and sufferings of this world fade away. Give me strength to withstand the training and discipline that will mold me into Your image.

100

When I Don't Understand Prayer

Lord, I know prayer is important. I think if I really understood what happened during prayer, I would be praying the way Paul said we should pray: without ceasing (1 Thessalonians 5:17). I honestly don't quite understand it…*but I want to*. Please teach me.

Sometimes You work in ways that we will never see, and for those times I pray for the gift of faith, to trust that You are moving even when I cannot see You. Lord, I know it's not just about the words I say; otherwise You wouldn't have given us the Lord's Prayer—so simple, so beautiful, so instructive. But in the Gospels, Jesus disappeared for days at a time to be alone with the Father in prayer. What were You saying, Jesus? How were You asking? What kind of conversations filled Your time in those long hours and sometimes days? Surely, the God who raised You from the dead can teach me how to converse with Him!

Jesus, I pray You would break down the judgmental voice in my head that tells me I'm not good at prayer. Allow my words to flow unhindered, as if I am talking with a friend. Protect my mind from any other voice that would seek to mimic You and confuse what the Holy Spirit is telling me. I thank You, Lord, that You welcome my prayers no matter how feeble they are. Thank You for walking alongside me as I learn. You are such a kind teacher.

When I Feel Like I Have Let God Down

God, I feel like I am constantly letting You down. My prayers have a theme. I come and confess the same things over and over. I struggle with recurring emotions. But then I look at Your Word: "For if, while we were God's enemies, we were reconciled to him through the death of his Son, how much more, having been reconciled, shall we be saved through his life!" (Romans 5:10).

Lord, You wooed me with Your unfailing love. That love was made available to me while I was still an enemy. What in the world makes me think You are constantly disappointed or angry with me now that I'm Your child? How much more pleased are You with me now as Your daughter than You were when I was a rebel? Lord, I reject the lies of the enemy that take my own self-judgment and project it onto You. I again submit myself to Your lordship, knowing that becoming like You through sanctification is a difficult process. I doubt I'll ever have a day when I don't have to submit some aspect of myself to Your perfect law of love, which casts out fear (1 John 4:18).

I refuse to allow the enemy's condemning words to beat me into submission to my sin. And I refuse to allow his hiss of condemnation to prevent me from pursuing You. I reject shame. I reject unhealthy striving. I release my imperfections and start afresh. I reject complacency and condemnation, for "there is now no condemnation for those who are in Christ Jesus" (Romans 8:1). I am resolved: "Forgetting what is behind and straining on toward what is ahead, I press on toward the goal to win the prize for which God has called me heavenward in Christ Jesus" (Philippians 3:13-14).

Section 9

WHEN. I. JUST. CAN'T. EVEN.

102

Courage for Being Misunderstood as a Christian

Lord, I know it shouldn't bother me, but I care about what other people think of me. I know that in other parts of the world, people are severely persecuted for the sake of Your name. They are willing and even called to lay down their very lives for You. My struggles have much smaller consequences, but those consequences still sting. Here I am, trying to be obedient to You—to lovingly but honestly speak truth into cultural issues—and I was laughed at today. They think I'm a religious nut. And if they don't think I'm crazy, they think I'm heartless. No matter how respectful I try to be, they are offended. I try to communicate clearly, but they misunderstand or misconstrue my words. They accuse me of hate, even as they hate me. Lord, I need Your courage. I want to please You more than man (Galatians 1:10). But my fear of backlash and vitriol is also real.

I'm scared of being snubbed by friends and family because I spoke truth. Lord, so many relationships are changing. Tension that wasn't there before now exists with people in my life. Following You is starting to cost more. I am afraid it is going to get worse. I need Your help to model courage for my little bears, because they are going to need it. Help me model Your heart so they know Your praise is worth more than any worldly approval they might have to give up. Help me equip them to stand on and for Your truth while still loving like Jesus. Help me inspire them to persevere and endure, even when following You is hard. Even when it hurts. Even when it's scary. Even when it's lonely. My prayer for my family is that we would be strong and courageous because You are with us when we follow You (Joshua 1:9). You will not leave us or forsake us (Deuteronomy 31:6). Please strengthen us, help us, and uphold us. Teach us to fear not (Isaiah 41:10).

Longing for Justice
in an Unjust World

Heavenly Father, it grieves me to see wickedness increase in Your perfectly created world. Things have gone terribly wrong, and they only seem to get worse with each passing day because we've abandoned Your truth and moral law. What You called good in the beginning is now called evil, and what is evil is now called good. Horrible acts of violence are committed against the most vulnerable image bearers. People mock You without suffering consequences for their actions, and I desperately want You to do something about it. In my limited understanding, I can't comprehend why You allow humans to seemingly go unpunished after committing such atrocious acts of injustice. But, Lord, what I do know is that You are good and Your Word is true. I can trust that, in the end, You will do what is right. Psalm 89:14 says, "Righteousness and justice are the foundation of your throne; love and faithfulness go before You." And Your Word confirms to me that You will not overlook injustice in the world forever. I am confident You are also able to use the evil deeds of wicked people to accomplish Your perfect plan.

If I am being honest, each sin I commit against one of my fellow image bearers—out of jealousy, selfishness, rage, or bitterness—is really against You, my holy God. I often fail to love people the way You have commanded, and that is rebellious and wrong. With the psalmist I confess that I have sinned against You alone, so You are right when You pass sentence and judge me (Psalm 51:4). Please create in me a clean heart and renew a steadfast spirit within me as I come before You in brokenness and humility (Psalm 51:10, 17). Thank You for providing an advocate in Jesus, who is perfectly righteous and comes before You on my behalf. Lord, I long for the day when You will restore all things and make everything as it should be once again. Until then, help me to trust Your perfect plan.

Honest RELEASE

While there is benefit to understanding what is going on in the world, we need to be careful not to focus too much on the brokenness. It steals our peace and robs our joy. Seek to be informed about the injustices in the world, but when you find yourself drowning in despair, choose to step away. Stay off social media. Turn off the news. Focus on what is within your control and not the things that aren't. We were never supposed to feel responsible for everything that happens in the world.

104

Loving like Jesus When the World Has Redefined Love

Lord, You say in Your Word that the two greatest commandments are to love You with all my heart, soul, mind, and strength, and to love others as myself (Mark 12:30-31). You tell us that the world will know we are Christians by our love (John 13:35). But God…I am so confused. My kids are so confused. The concept of love has been co-opted to mean basically anything anyone wants. My children want to love like Jesus loved, loving the unlovable and being a champion for those who are suffering. But how can I teach them what true love *is* when the world's definition is so different?

Teach me to model true love. May I be patient without enabling. May I be kind without compromising truth. Lord, may I not envy when others have (or seem to have) something I lack—whether that be position, privilege, or possessions. And God, may I never flaunt what I have and tempt others to envy me. Lord, may I never see my gifts and talents as making me more or less than others. When I am annoyed, may I counter it with Your grace. May I seek Your best for others even *more* than they do for themselves, or even when they see Your best as oppressive.

Oh my God, when the world tells me it is "loving" while embracing lies, may I refuse to participate, even when I am called names for doing so. May I rejoice whenever I see truth being proclaimed and help others to see the beauty of truth. God, You are the way, the truth, and the life, and Your Word is truth (John 14:6; 17:17). May I absorb the blows that are aimed at Your image bearers without retaliating or growing bitter.

May I always believe that Your hand is not too short to save, and remind me that nobody is beyond Your grace. May I always point people to the glory that awaits them despite the hardships of this world, and may I be an agent of encouragement to those enduring hardships by helping to carry their burdens (Galatians 6:2). Help me endure the sorrows of this world, knowing that endurance produces perseverance, which produces character, which produces hope for the glory to come—and that hope will never disappoint (Romans 5:3-5). Your love never ends. When I feel tempted to compromise on any point, direct me back to Your definition of love (1 Corinthians 13:4-8).

_____

_____

_____

_____

_____

_____

_____

_____

_____

_____

_____

_____

_____

_____

_____

_____

_____

_____

_____

When My Kids Are So Loud, Needy, and Whiny That I Want to Scream

Goldfish crackers. The crusts on the bread this way, not that way. "Pick me up." "Put me down." The right pacifier. The right stuffed animal. God, I feel like I am the deputy director of a million things that seem trivial, but which seem to determine whether my kids will have a meltdown or not. I cannot keep track of it all. I cannot handle the whining, the screaming, and the tears and their endless clawing at me for more, more, more. More attention. More energy. More of me when I feel like I am spent. I feel as though I have nothing left. Lord, I used to have a life where I dealt with things that seemed more important. I confess, God, that I sometimes want to just scream in their faces, "Leave me alone!" "Find it yourself." "Make it yourself." "Do it yourself." But they can't, Lord. I wish they could, but they can't.

I need You, God. I am exhausted all the time, and I can't point to a single thing I accomplished today that feels meaningful.

I am about to lose it, Father, so I choose right now to shut my mouth. Quiet my heart, Lord. Help me stop my own whining and return to what is true. Help me to see that all of this matters because my children matter. Show me that all of these tiny sacrifices are reinforcing in them that they have a mother who cares about what matters to them. And I pray that my caring about what matters to them will one day translate into them knowing they can trust You because their cares and concerns matter to You too. For that reason, I will never stop caring. I will never stop giving. I will never stop doing the job You have called me to do.

God, I choose to be still in this moment—despite their cries in the background—and meditate on this truth: reminding myself of why I do what I do You are pleased with me in this moment. Oh Lord, I hope You are pleased with my every effort to love and care for these children that You have blessed me with, and Your pleasure has an eternal weight to it. With Your help, all things can be done for Your glory, God. Thank You for this reminder. When the enemy comes and tries to spread his lies again, I pray that I can return to this moment, to this truth, and pick up my cross. I know this stage will not last forever.

I thank You, Lord, for the honor of being faithful in the little things, knowing that the little things are never little to You. Give me the energy to continue through this day, and God, please give me a deep sleep tonight that will refresh me for another day of the same.

Honest IDEA

Susanna Wesley (John Wesley's mother) had nine children in a small house. She was known for throwing her apron over her head when she had reached her limit and needed alone time. The kids knew that if Mom's apron was over her head, you left her *alone*. Moms often need a time-out as much as kids. Take a leaf from Susanna Wesley's book and allow yourself a space—like a special chair—where your kids know that you are in time-out. Unless someone is positively dying, whatever they want for that moment can wait.

106

When I Want to Run Away from My Responsibilities

Oh God, I need You right now. I feel broken, bloodied, and bruised. I feel overwhelmed with too many tasks and incapable of doing them all well. I feel like if someone puts one more thing on my shoulders, I'll break. Then I get loaded down with one more thing…and another…and another. My body is tired. My mind cannot focus. I can no longer tell the difference between what *feels* real and what *is* real.

I imagine myself running away from all my responsibilities, but there is no freedom in that either. Because when I stop and think about it, I love the tasks You have given me. My job, my family, my children, and all that comes with them are blessings from You. Even when I cannot see it, You tell me I am the one You have chosen for this role. Your righteous right hand will uphold me (Isaiah 41:10). Oh God, plant that knowledge deep in my heart. I pray that I would feel Your strength flowing into me. And in the times when I can't feel it, I pray You would endow me with a special abundance of faith.

Am I Doing Enough?

Lord, I sometimes feel so guilty that I'm not doing enough. I'm not volunteering at homeless shelters. I'm not working a food bank. I'm not even teaching Sunday school. I wonder if I'm only doing the "good works" that I feel comfortable with, and when I get to heaven one day, You'll just look at me with a massive facepalm, wondering how I missed so much of what You said.

Help me to give myself grace when even the load I already carry feels too heavy. Motherhood *is* constant service. I pray You would silence the voice in my head that tells me my contributions are not enough. Thank You that I am only held accountable for how I use the time, energy, and resources You have given me; I am not measured against how others use what You've provided to them. When my children watch me, may they notice how I serve them, how I treat their father, and how I use my time. The day will come when I can take on more; this is just a difficult season of parenting. In the meantime, open my eyes to the needs I *can* meet. Show me things I can do with my children so that my service becomes another facet in their discipleship training.

Honest STEP

I (Hillary) had a mother who loved to cook, and I remember her taking me (as a preschooler) along with her to deliver food to the sick through Meals on Wheels. Think of an activity that you enjoy and that blesses people, where your kids can serve alongside you. It can be a fond memory for them that they will remember (and hopefully mimic) when they have their own children.

108

Postpartum Anxiety

God, I can't do this. I need You to step in. I have so many people supporting me, yet I feel so alone. The room was spinning when I tried to rock my baby to sleep; I'm that tired. I want to leave the house; staying home is exhausting. I can't handle the nightmares and waking up night after night in a cold sweat worried that my child's not breathing. I'm up countless times during the night checking on [him/her]. God, will You watch my child breathe for me? I need sleep. I can't leave the house, though; it's too hard and too scary. What if my child falls? What if I drop [him/her]?

I need help. I can't be in charge of this person. I love [him/her] endlessly, but I feel so detached. Where is that instant maternal bond everyone told me about? I love this child, but I just want someone else to take care of [him/her]. Where are You? I need You. I know You're here, but I don't feel You. Help me feel You. I want to want You more. I want to trust You more. But right now, I don't. Wipe away my endless tears and wake me up from this nightmare. God, help me. Help my child. Take care of us.

Please be with my husband as he feels helpless. Where else can we turn, Lord, but to You? Point us to angels of mercy—doctors and counselors who will help us make it through this nightmarish season. Give me the courage to ask for help; it's the best thing I can do for myself and my child. Lord, give us peace.

God, help me remember this is just a season and it won't last forever. Give me strength to push back against the lie that I am alone. I'm not; others have gone through this, and You are always with me. Your Word says You care for the lilies of the field and the sparrows in the sky (Matthew 6:25-34). Remind me how much more you care for me, for us, as Your children. You will empower me to do that which You have given me to do. God, keep the truths coming.

If you are struggling with postpartum depression or anxiety at any level, you are not alone. Confide in your loved ones, and talk with an ob-gyn or midwife who understands the complexities and has treated postpartum symptoms. Make sure you have at least one person who will hold you accountable until you get the help you need.

Postpartum Depression

Lord, it's not supposed to be like this. Surely it's not. Everyone else talks about amazing bonds with their babies, and I feel nothing. Whose child is this? [He/She] can't be mine. [He/She] didn't come from my body. Someone, take this baby away. I can't do this. How can I do this when I can't even feel love or receive love? I just want to lie on the floor and cry. Taking care of [him/her] is too hard; it hurts too much. But I feel judged when others try to take care of [him/her] for me.

At the smallest provocations, intense anger starts taking over my body and my mind. I am scared of driving everyone away. And yet I also want to be alone. But I don't. God, this is not the righteousness You desire. I know this is probably hormones, but when they are going so crazy, I can't even think straight. I feel like I'm losing my mind. God, I need You. I need You to remind me of truth. I need You to tell me I'm not alone. I need to be able to *feel* like I'm not alone. Lord, where are You? Please be here. You say in Your Word that You will never leave me or forsake me. How do I focus on this truth when I can't feel it?

Oh God, speed up time. Take me through this trial and bring me out whole on the other side. In Your power, keep me from doing something I'll regret. I can't handle this fear and this sadness. At moments I feel like I don't want to be here anymore. But no, I refuse to entertain those thoughts. Lord, I cling to Your truth. All I can do is repeat it over and over. My life has purpose. You have chosen me to be the mother of this child. I *am* the mother of this child. Hold me in your arms as I hold [him/her] in mine.

Give those around me a super indwelling of grace while I am recovering. I need sleep. Help me to sleep. You are right here with me, God. Please get me the help I need even though I am too tired to ask for it.

Surround me with people who will physically pick me up and get me where I need to go for help and healing. Keep reminding me that You are with me, and this won't last forever.

Honest STEP

Please review the Honest Step under the prayer for "Postpartum Anxiety" on page 170.

110

When I Feel like the Wrong Mom for the Job

Heavenly Father, I don't feel equipped to be a good mom today. I was too irritable, too harsh, and I just want to hide from my kids. The enemy wants me to believe my children would be better off with a different mother—that they need a mother who only feeds them organic snacks, who never raises her voice, or who has an endless attention span. They need a mom who never gets tired or frustrated.

I don't want shame to win today. You have called me to this role, which means You will equip me for it. Thank You for new mercies every morning (Lamentations 3:22-23). Thank You for the gift and calling of being a mother. Thank You for my little blessings. Thank You for the truth that when I am weak, You are strong (2 Corinthians 12:10). When I am empty, You fill me.

Lord, I surrender myself to You once again. Let my kids see a mama who is always reliant upon her heavenly Father. Please help me to represent You to my children by showing them Your patience, Your steadfastness, and Your grace.

God, help me learn to give myself grace as well. Thankfully, You are a God who does not waste anything. You can even use today's shortcomings toward tomorrow's victories. My children can learn more from watching me navigate my mistakes than they ever would if I made motherhood look easy. So, God, I praise You even in my failures.

111

Praying Through Exhaustion

Dear Lord, thank You so much for the blessing of being a mother. I know that right now, I stand where I once only prayed to be. You in Your infinite wisdom gave me these children in Your timing, and I trust You, but I'm still struggling.

I'm afraid to even speak this out loud because I'm ashamed of how I feel. Too often, I feel like I am at my breaking point. I'm worn down by trying to raise these children well. This stage of motherhood seems beyond my strength and understanding. I feel like I'm failing before breakfast. I never knew motherhood could be so incredibly hard. Even though I love my children dearly, I wasn't prepared for the 24-7 nature of parenting. And at night, I drop into bed exhausted and defeated. But I don't want to just survive these hard days. I want to thrive. I want to be known for Your peace and patience instead of my stress and anxiety. I need Your presence and encouragement to keep me from being crushed by the hamster wheel of my kids' schedules. Help me recognize when I'm taking on burdens and expectations I was never meant to carry. Please help me ignore the messages of this world, which tell me that my day is never done. May I instead dwell in the richness of Your grace and Sabbath rest.

I need You to give me supernatural strength for the tiring moments, patience for the frustrating ones, and joy in the more monotonous tasks of homemaking and mothering. Please help me disciple my children, not just discipline them. I know You love me when I'm at my lowest just as much as my highest. Help me love my children the same way.

Remind me to be present in everyday moments. May I relish the ways motherhood is refining and growing me. Help me remember the messes and chores mean my home and heart are full.

Asking the Holy Spirit to Help Me Pray

Lord, I confess I don't know how to pray for this situation. My words don't even form; they just come out as a guttural cry, and I feel overwhelmed. It's all too much. But You have been faithful in the past, so I am asking You to be faithful again. Your Word tells me Your Holy Spirit is my helper, and when I do not know how I ought to pray, Your Spirit Himself intercedes for me (Romans 8:26). Please do that now.

Teach me to be intentional, partnering always with Your Spirit, asking for help in every situation, and bringing all requests and petitions to You. I feel so discouraged right now, but I choose to place my hope in You. May I walk closely with the Holy Spirit as I go about my day, moving forward in wisdom and clear thinking because You transform my mind (Romans 12:2).

Holy Spirit, help me in my weakness. All around me, evil seems to triumph and the wicked continue to prosper. The world I was born into no longer exists. But for my children and their children, I do not want to give up on praying, asking for what has been lost and broken to be restored. But when my prayers feel futile and words will not come, Holy Spirit, please intercede for me. When all I have to give are tears, and when my thoughts and feelings cannot be put into human terms, thank You for giving me Your words. As I seek to remain steadfast in prayer, please continue to search my heart and guide me in lifting up this situation in accordance with the will of the Father.

When God Feels Silent

Father, I'm praying but I hear nothing. I feel nothing. I don't think You are ignoring me, for You tell me You know the number of hairs on my head (Luke 12:7). Not even a sparrow falls to the ground without Your knowledge (Matthew 10:29). You are an infinite God, which means You have an infinite amount of attention to give Your creation. When I sit and when I rise, when I bless and when I curse, Your eyes are fixed on me. So why can't I hear You?

Could it be that my ears have grown so accustomed to the manic noise of this world that I have dulled my ability to hear from You? Have I become conditioned to the world's constant activity and endless distraction? As I squirm in the silence, I am reminded to cease my striving and to be still before You (Psalm 46:10). Your silence is not from lack of attention. I may not hear You, Lord, but You have not forgotten me. When Your silence feels unbearable, I pray for Your calming hand to soothe my ever-active brain. When I feel like I can do anything but be still, may You provide ways to foster stillness. God, we are such a task-oriented, *now, now, now* world. Please give me the self-control and patience to wait on Your voice when it doesn't feel like it is coming fast enough.

Honest EVALUATION

Ask God to reveal to you if anything is keeping you from hearing Him—an unconfessed sin, busyness, a cluttered mind? Sometimes it's none of the above. Don't be afraid of the silence, but be persistent in prayer.

114

God, Please Use a Megaphone

God, the Bible tells us that You sometimes speak in a still small voice—that You aren't necessarily in the tornadoes, the rainstorms, the lightning, or the hail. At times, You are the quiet whisper (1 Kings 19:11-12). But honestly, with the noise and the chaos of little kids running around and everything else going on, I can't hear any whispers. I'm really going to need that giant megaphone voice from heaven telling me, "Do this!" or "Do that!"

I need clear direction. I need clear guidance. And yet I know Your will isn't always just one thing. So Lord, bring me godly counsel, the wisdom of Your Word, and the knowledge of when I have the freedom to move ahead in a variety of directions as long as I'm within the latitude of Your moral will. You delight in our decisions, so please keep me from making a really dumb one. Nail doors shut if they need to be shut. And if a door needs to be opened, Lord…use dynamite to blow that sucker open.

I want to hear You more clearly. I want to do Your will, but so often I feel like I'm blindly stumbling along and hoping to be in the general vicinity of the right path. Yet You say You give wisdom "generously to all without finding fault" (James 1:5). Please help me hear You in whatever way You choose to speak, trusting that even when it feels like a guessing game, I hear You more than I realize. In hindsight, I can often tell where Your hand was at work and where You guided me, but I need a little extra hand-holding right now. I trust that I'll look back and see Your providence and goodness during this time as well.

(Review the Honest Journaling on the next page.)

Honest JOURNALING

Keep a written record of when God has led you and when you have heard His voice—even if you didn't realize it until after the fact. When you are tempted to think He is silent, this will help remind yourself of the many ways He has led you in the past.

115

When My Anxiety About the World Rubs Off on My Child

Dear God, I'm anxious about the state of our world, and it's rubbing off on my kids. Every day I read more bad news, more stories that sicken or anger me, and they put me in a funk. I vocalize my concerns to my husband while little ears are listening, which often is not wise. My kids are not growing up in the same kind of world I did, and they know it. It worries them, Lord, and it worries me too.

Please give me wisdom to navigate this "new" world with my kids. I know You give wisdom to those who ask, Lord, and oh, how I need it (James 1:5)! Help me also to hold my tongue when I'm around my children so as to not worry them with things too great for their little hearts to bear (Proverbs 21:23). Turn me away from my phone and television and instead to Your Word (Psalm 119:28). Give me peace, calmness, and confidence that You are on Your throne, in complete control (Psalm 103:19). Help me to not be anxious about tomorrow, next week, or next year, and may the peace that overcomes me wash over my kids too (Philippians 4:6-7). I don't want them to be anxious, Lord, so please calm my anxious heart. And in those times when my children's anxiety isn't secondhand, when the world itself overwhelms them and tries to steal their joy, make them resilient, faithful, and strong. I trust You, Lord, with the hearts of my children.

Honest STEP

Take a look at Philippians 4:8. When you and your kids find yourselves overwhelmed by the world, pick one of the words in the verse. Then brainstorm as many fun things as you can that fit the description. From chattering squirrels to fresh lemonade—nothing delightful is off the table!

When I Can't Focus on My Bible Reading

Father, I'm sitting here trying to get into the Word, but my mind keeps going in a million different directions. It's like my brain is working on overdrive, trying to find something (anything!) else to do. I don't understand it. *Why* is this such a battle?

There are so many times when I walk away from Your Word feeling refreshed, refilled, and ready to conquer the day. And then there are days like today…when reading Your Word feels like a total chore. I didn't hear anything specific, and I don't feel like I've learned anything in particular. It is just a check mark on my to-do list. I know not every Bible reading will offer some huge epiphany, but neither is every meal I eat a culinary masterpiece. Nourishment is nourishment, even if I don't feel it immediately.

When I am distracted, delete those thoughts from my head. When I am unfocused, draw me back in. Even when reading Scripture just feels like a duty, may I delight in the obedience of the act and feel Your pleasure at my perseverance. And may I remember that just because I don't feel "changed" doesn't mean I am *not* changed by this small act of faithfulness. Lord, please give me an insatiable craving for the Word. I cannot change my own heart or desires, but You can. I thank You for delighting in my attempts, no matter how feeble.

Honest IDEA

When your brain is going in all directions, read out loud. It is harder to space out, and you have the multisensory experience of seeing, speaking, and hearing. If you are having trouble concentrating because you keep having to-do items interjecting themselves, we have found it helpful to keep a list of those items on a separate sheet of paper.

Section 10

PRAYERS YOU PRAY
YOU NEVER HAVE TO PRAY

Marriage in Crisis

Lord, my husband and I have not been connecting well lately. If we're not fighting, we're silently growing apart, and I don't know which is worse. I'm angry about so many things, and yet I know I'm not innocent either. I have been short with him. I have been disrespectful. [Insert your own confessions.]

Lord, I pray for protection over our marriage. The enemy wants to exploit times like this, to tempt us to imagine life apart. I pray we would be able to talk things out and expose them to the open air. Give us the patience and fortitude to work through our problems, no matter how relieving it might be to look elsewhere for attention.

God, You joined us together in marriage; we are one flesh. I pray against anything that would tear us apart. I pray especially against [things you see coming between you and your husband].

Lord, I don't want to hurt anymore. I am tempted to protect my heart by becoming cold and indifferent toward [husband], but that is not the way to reconcile. Please give me strength to still be vulnerable with him and he with me. Grant me courage to overcome my fears: fear of losing my husband, fear of being with my husband and staying this unhappy, fear that things will change, fear that they won't.

I fall before You, God, unable to stand. With every fault I find in him, I know I could find ten in me. I want to be patient, but I don't want to act like everything is fine when it's not. I need You, Lord, to show me the right balance. Show me when to speak up and when to be silent. Teach me to absorb, but also how to righteously stand up for myself. Show me how to have mercy without enabling. And God, convict me when I have gone too far to one side or the other. Protect me from myself. Give me discernment to know if the marriage has gone from difficult to dangerous for me and the kids.

Lord God, *Jehovah-rapha*, the God who heals, I pray You would heal our marriage. I will pray for it every day that I have breath. And when I feel like I can't even breathe, may Your Spirit breathe through me. Please remind my husband why he married me, and remind me of why I married him. I pray You would protect both of us from the false promises of divorce. The grass is rarely greener. Make us a family again. Make us tender again. You can bring dry bones to life, God (Ezekiel 37). Please return life to this dying marriage. Do what only You can do.

Honest REMINDER

A difficult marriage is not the same thing as an abusive marriage. If you find yourself unable to tell the difference, please seek the guidance of a trained professional who knows the difference between difficult and dangerous. (And be aware, pastors are not always the best trained for this. Find someone who will fight for the permanency of marriage, but not at the expense of abuse victims.)

Death of Husband

Oh God, my God, this isn't the way it was supposed to be! My chest hurts. A lead weight is ripping the breath from my lungs. I can't stop screaming. My body is heavy with grief.

God, I don't know how to survive the next 20 minutes, much less the next 20 years. I want to know how to trust Your perfect timing and Your will even in this, but it's so hard. I'm so angry with You for allowing him to die! I can't understand. I don't know if I'll ever understand. Hold me tight even as I flail and punch and kick in this painful rage. And when I shut down, unable to carry the emotional load, wrap me in Your comfort and fill me with Your strength. Give me purpose. Help me put one foot in front of the other even when I want to crawl into a ball and hide from the world. My children still need me, God. I cannot disappear on them.

Abba Father, help me process my anger while also remembering Your goodness. Give me the ability to love and trust You when I can't move forward on my own. You can bring beauty from ashes (Isaiah 61:3). Please help me see glimpses of Your redemption through this tragedy in our lives so I can stand in this storm. You are the one who the wind and waves obey (Matthew 8:27). And I'm clinging to that when I can't cling to anything else.

Fill me with Your supernatural strength as I navigate losing the love of my life. Give me clarity of mind as I deal with mounds of legalities and financial concerns. Grant me humility to seek and accept help from those You've placed around me. Allow me to grieve well in front of my children; let them see me cry and still get up and live.

Even as I'm crushed by sorrow, help me model perseverance. And let me demonstrate leaning on You through it all, even though I don't understand why this happened. Help us all to trust in Your love and mercy through this difficult time.

Give me peace and patience to parent grieving children who often act defiantly or disobediently in their pain. Allow me to see beyond harsh words and behaviors to address their hearts in ways that draw them to You. Give us grace toward each other; none of us is at our best right now. Strengthen our relationship through this tragedy, and help us process this pain in ways that draw us closer to each other and to You.

Lord, it was never Your desire for me to be a single parent, but You allow things to happen in Your perfect wisdom. I don't know how we will manage. I don't know how to run a household alone, much less lead our family. I can't be both mother and father, but I'm asking You to supernaturally help me do and be all the things my family needs. Lord, place godly men around our family to be pillars of strength when we need them in the coming years. We will feel my husband's absence for decades to come. Please hold us close when we miss him the most.

Someday soon, remind us to embrace life again and to celebrate his memory with joy and laughter. Be gracious to us in our grief. We cannot do this without You.

Honest JOURNALING

Everyone deals with grief differently. Journal through what you are feeling, and add it into your prayers. Allow it all to come out before the Lord.

119

For the Unequally Yoked Mama Bear (or the Mama Bear Whose Husband Has Left the Faith)

Heavenly Father, rescue my husband from doubt, as You did me. Please set him beside me to lead our family by following You. This is just too much for me to do by myself; this world is too hard. It's against us. It's against our kids. It wants their hearts and their minds, and that is scary. I wear myself out working to teach and train them every day, but I am battling from all sides. It is painfully hard doing this alone. I find myself envying Christian couples who are working seamlessly side by side, husband and wife, with the shared mission of training up their children. The lies of this world are insidious, tempting, and so deceitful. And honestly, I am just tired. It is my joy to do the work of discipling my kids, but it is exhausting to do it by myself.

Near-terror grips my heart as I imagine my children older, exposed to the darkness of our culture, faced with the choice to love You and be hated by this world or to conform. How I long for my babies to witness their parents united together in their pursuit of a life that honors You. I wish they had us both in their corner, praying for them and supporting them in the Lord. But we are a house divided now, God. Can I give them this foundation on my own?

Father, I beg You, don't let go of my kids. And don't let go of my husband. Draw his heart near to You. Help him to forgive the hurt in his past. Restore his faith in You and Your church. Soften his heart and remove the bitterness that plagues him. My kids need a father who loves You. I need a husband who follows You. But as I wait, help me to remember that I am not working alone, but with You as my guide. And while I am powerless, You are not. Provide me with the energy to persevere as I disciple our children on my own. Redeem these years where my husband and I are not living as one. Let my kids see him struggle and then return to You, able to better answer their questions and objections. You are not a God of fear, but a God of joy, and my joy is in You no matter the circumstances. Father, save us. My trust is in You alone. You are good. And I pray Your will be done.

Cries of a Single Mama Bear

Oh God, there are days when I am so joyful. The kids are behaving, and I don't feel like I'm drowning. And then there are days like today, when I don't feel like I can do this anymore. Lord, how much have I deprived my kids by not providing them with a home that has both parents under the same roof? The voice of the accuser is constantly whispering condemnation in my ears, reminding me of every way I have failed. I cannot be both mother and father. I try to be both, but I am not enough—despite what all those stupid slogans say.

I see what other kids are able to do with two parents in the home, and I feel so guilty that I have not given my children that experience. Oh God, please take away these feelings of guilt and shame. I know they are not from You. I release them to You, reminding myself that there is therefore no condemnation for those who are in Christ Jesus (Romans 8:1). I reject the voice of condemnation, and I receive Your grace.

God, remind me of how you can bring about good in *every* situation (Romans 8:28). I thank You for providing generously where we are lacking (Philippians 4:19). I pray for strong male mentors for my children who will fill some of the void left from their father. I pray for a strong relationship between my children and their father; help me hold my tongue when I want to criticize him and rejoice in whatever ways he is part of their lives.

Especially, God, I pray for this never-ending longing for companionship and intimacy with a man. You say it is not good for man (or woman!) to be alone, yet here I am. I am in the one state you called "not good." I know, Lord, You will provide for all my needs, and I thank You for the ways You meet me here in my loneliness. You fill me with Yourself. But God, I am so overwhelmed with desire for a partner in life. I want to give myself, body and soul, to a man who loves me, but You have not yet brought him to me.

188 • ||||||||||||||||||||||||

Lord, I pray this godly discontentment will not give the enemy a foothold. Do not let my unmet desires blossom into bitterness against You. Oh God, You never promised me a spouse as a reward for being faithful. A husband is not something I can "earn" by being good enough or spiritual enough or content enough. If I am still single, it is not because You have forgotten me. For whatever reason, You are allowing me to walk this road—and despite my feelings, I vow to trust in Your plans, even when I don't understand them. You have promised me Yourself, Lord, and I want that to be enough. I pray I would be able to lean into that. These longings for a husband may never fully go away, but I pray my joy in You would eclipse even these healthy, God-given desires.

Lord, meet me when I am at my wits' end. Provide for me financially when the numbers just aren't adding up. You are refining me through these lessons in faith, and while they are hard, I receive them (Job 2:10). God, I still pray You would provide me with a husband who can help shoulder the load. But beyond that, let me be faithful with what I have, knowing You do not judge me according to anyone else's situation, but mine alone. I trust that where I am weak, You are strong (2 Corinthians 12:9-10). Oh Lord, be my rock, my provider, and the love that sustains me.

Child Comes Out as LGBTQ+

Lord, I feel like my breath has been knocked out of my body. I don't understand what has happened. God, [child] has come out to us as [gay, trans, bi, etc.]. This is hitting closer to home than I ever expected. I know this happens, but I never thought it would be us—not our family. Lord, I place myself on Your altar, releasing my heartache, my fear, my disappointment, my anger—whatever my first instincts are. The voice of condemnation is telling me it's all my fault. If only I had noticed this or done that. Every parenting mistake I've ever made is racing across my mind, and I don't know if I can shoulder the weight of this responsibility.

Oh God, first and foremost, please speak Your truth to my grieving heart. I pray for the supernatural gift of listening. May I seek to understand [child] before I try to lecture [him/her]. God, this announcement has not come out of nowhere. I pray for an unflinching face as I seek to discuss how [he/she] came to this conclusion about [his/her] identity. Lord, I know that [child] has been told by the LGBTQ+ community that I will rage at, reject, hate, or disown [him/her] because, heartbreakingly, many Christian parents have not reacted well to similar announcements from their children. But I pray that any fleshly reactions I have would be silenced by love—both mine and Yours—for [child]. Where there is pain and hurt, I pray I would seek to understand. Where there is rebellion, I pray that I would allow You to be the Holy Spirit in [his/her] life.

Let nothing take precedence over the time I need to spend guiding [child] through this trial—not a job, not a school schedule, not a college education, *nothing*. If [he/she] is still under our roof, give me insight to recognize which influences are speaking deceptions to [him/her]. If needed, help me to remove [him/her] from any spaces where those harmful lies are promoted. God, let my actions come from love for my child and trust in Your power, rather than from fear and the misbelief that my child's fate is something I can control. Though I will do everything I can to help [child], I know that, ultimately, [his/her] future belongs to You alone.

God, show me what to do as we move forward with [child's] announcement. The enemy takes every idea I have and reminds me of the thousands of ways it could blow up in my face. I feel paralyzed with fear of doing something wrong, reacting wrong, blaming the wrong things, not listening well enough, or pushing [him/her] further away from You. Oh God, I lay myself prostrate before You, knowing my relationship with [child] will change. But loving [him/her] through this is *not* one of those ways. Show me what is within my power and what is not.

Lord, I know this is the beginning of a long spiritual battle for my child. I pray against the lies that [child] has believed about [his/her] identity and sexuality. May [he/she] remember that we all have sin that weighs us down. No one is excused from dying to their desires. I pray against the lie that sexuality is the only area that doesn't have to be surrendered at the foot of the cross.

God, I pray You would protect my motherly instinct, which tells me to change my theology about sexuality in order to maintain peace with my child. No matter how much I seek to love [child], my relationship with *You* is still my highest priority, because abiding in You will always lead to *more* grace, *more* love, *more* truth, *more* gentleness, and *more* kindness, not less. If I see myself wavering in these areas, help me to identify the lies or fears that are getting in the way of Your fruits. Give me the strength to continue fighting for [child] even when [he/she] wishes I would not. Give me the steadfastness to pray, even when it doesn't seem like anything is happening. Give me the wisdom to know what love looks like in each situation. Surround me with a supportive community that will encourage me both in my love for my child and my commitment to Your Word. Oh God, heal my grieving mama's heart. You are close to the brokenhearted and save those who are crushed in spirit (Psalm 34:18). Be near me now, my God.

Honest RESOURCE

If you have a loved one struggling with sexuality, we recommend the ministry Living Hope. You can find them at livehope.org.

122

Pornography Addiction in the Home

Oh God. This was never supposed to happen to our family. Pornography has entered our home and has taken root. Lord God, [person] is powerless against it. There is so much shame. There is so much hurt. God, we need Your freedom in this place.

You say in the Sermon on the Mount that if our eye causes us to sin, pluck it out (Mark 9:47). Lord, give us the courage to do whatever needs to be done to cut this addiction off at its roots, even if it means getting rid of internet and smartphones in the house. Give me the fortitude, ability, and resources to set boundaries and stick to them. I know that [person] may still find ways to access pornography, but at least I will know in my heart that I have done everything I could to keep it out of our home.

Lord, Satan has a foothold wherever Your good gift of sexuality is distorted. This pornography addiction has allowed unclean spirits into our home. I don't know how to close all the spiritual doors that this perversion has opened. God, I pray special protection over the others in our home who are experiencing the spiritual ramifications of pornography. Even when the kids don't know what is going on, they can feel it. I see them affected by a darkness they cannot see or name.

I pray for my husband to take seriously his role as spiritual protector of our home. May he take the initiative to combat whatever is making porn possible here in our sanctuary. And where he refuses to exercise his authority, God, please come and be our protector.

Most of all, I pray against the lust, disconnection, and despair that have driven [person] to believe the lie that momentary pleasure can cure their wounded heart. God, I know so much of pornography addiction goes beyond lust. Addiction is real. Addiction is physical.

And addiction is spiritual. I pray for healthy connections and for trust to be regrown. I pray You would mend the chemicals that have been altered in [person's] brain. Lord, send people to [person] to hold [him/her] accountable. I pray that shame would not have a foothold here because we are willing to speak into the light that which has been done in the darkness. I pray for the boldness to confess, openly and willingly, with the spiritual mentors in our lives, so they may direct us toward help. I pray for those in spiritual authority over [person] to courageously confront and hold [him/her] accountable.

Get this sin out of our camp, Lord, and reestablish a home of peace. Where this addiction has wrecked relationships among our family, I pray You would restore and renew our commitment to one another. I pray for the voice of condemnation to give way to Your sweet call to repentance.

Honest RESOURCE

If you or someone you love is struggling with a porn addiction, we recommend Fight the New Drug. You can find them at fightthenewdrug.org.

123

Wife of an Addict

Lord, help my husband break free from his addiction. As long as his addiction persists, his brain is enslaved. He hides it from me by telling lies, but this is hurtful and diminishes my role as his helper. Allow me to see through his deceptions so I am not blindsided and living in a constant state of betrayal and grief. I already don't trust him, and it wreaks havoc on our marriage.

Lord, take this burden from me; I cannot be the guardian of his reputation while still trying to protect our children. Show me safe places to get help as our family suffers from the consequences of his sin. Help me to set boundaries that don't enable his addiction. Hold me up when the kids and I aren't incentive enough for him to break free; comfort us with the reassurance of Your love, and remind us that our worth is not diminished by his seeming disregard. Guard my children, Lord. Please spare them from the fallout of his behavior, and keep them out of harm's way.

Give him the strength and desire to place his addiction wholly into Your hands. Replace his addiction with a desire to be connected to You and his family. Sustain him when he feels weak. Send him strong people who will tell him the tough things he needs to hear. Make them compassionate enough to not shame him when he backslides. Please protect him from the lie that just because he fails once, he is doomed to fail every time. Let the Holy Spirit prompt him to confess his urges and weaknesses instead of hiding behind spiritual fig leaves. Give me discernment on how to move forward within this broken marriage or when I need to prioritize the protection of the kids. Help me to continue to grow in faith with You, even as my faith in my husband is damaged.

Pregnancy Loss

Dear God, why? Why did I have to lose this precious baby? I don't understand. So many women are choosing to end the life of their unborn, but I wanted this baby. I prayed for this baby. So many girls and women get pregnant before they're ready, but I prepared my life, my home, and my marriage for this child. None of it makes sense to me, but I know You are good. You have given me enough reasons to trust in Your character even when I share in the tormenting pain of this fallen world.

I just want to get to my baby. I don't want to end my life, Lord, but I want to see my baby. Please let me dream about this child, to see my child with You. My job was to take care of [him/her]; I want to do my job. But I know You designed this baby, know this baby, and even loved this baby better than I ever could. And I thank You for keeping my child safe with You.

I feel turned inside out. Please put the right people in my life and give them the words that will comfort me. So many people mean well, but their words are like salt in an open wound. Let me survive this. Please give me strong enough relationships with people who can withstand whatever ugliness grief brings out of me. May I not judge myself, but neither let me stop apologizing when I know I have acted unfairly toward someone who was trying to comfort me. Do not allow my other relationships to unravel while I fight drowning under these waves of sorrow. It's so hard to be graceful and authentic, because the authentic me wants to scream and do something rash. Please give me self-control when I feel I have none. You, Jesus, are the Prince of Peace. Let Your Spirit descend upon me and work within me so I may show its fruit.

Give me rest and healing. This roller coaster of hormones is torture; the emotional turmoil is exhausting. I feel like my body is being pumped with drugs stronger than I can physically handle, but I know You are faithful to hear my cry for physical restoration.

Please let this situation have a greater purpose. Show me where the loss of this tiny life had meaning and impact. I know You have the power to use any circumstance to bring about glory for Your kingdom. Do not let this story end here. Let me see the good that can come out of this tragedy. All I can see is my pain right now.

I know You are faithful to hear the prayers of those who love You. I know I am Your own child, and Your motivation was not one of malice when You allowed me to experience this. Don't let me go, God. Keep me near You. Help me think clearly. Carry me.

For My Prodigal Child in Rebellion

Lord, You love [child] even more than I do. All I've ever wanted was to lead [him/her] in Your ways. I thought we did everything right. I prayed for [him/her], protected [him/her], pointed [him/her] to You. But it wasn't enough. Oh God, why wasn't I enough? [Child] has rejected You. [He/she] has rejected me. [He/she] has rejected [his/her] father. There's nothing left that I can do—so I release [him/her] to [his/her] own folly and whatever consequences come with it. Give me the strength to allow [child] to temporarily go through hell on earth, if that's what it takes for [him/her] to spend eternity with You.

I pray that whatever [child] indulges in will not bring [him/her] comfort. I pray [he/she] would not know a moment of peace while walking in opposition to You. Lord, may [he/she] never fit in with groups [he/she] is trying to join. Let the sins [child] revels in ultimately nauseate [him/her]. I pray that no matter how far [he/she] runs, that [he/she] would not be able to outrun the voice of Your Holy Spirit, calling [him/her], wooing [him/her] back to You.

God, I pray special protection over our family. Protect us from judgmental looks of those in our family and our church. Please bring me prayer partners who want to help and not judge. I don't want to feel so isolated. Help us when [my husband] and I are tempted to blame each other. Oh God, protect our relationship. Pease don't let my child's actions steal my marriage too. Let us travel this path together, weathering the storm. And please protect my other children, that [child's] actions against You would not spread to them.

God, I need You to take from me this overwhelming sense of responsibility. I am so tired of trying to save [child]. I do not know what releasing [him/her] will mean. Jail? Hospital? Living on the street?

Oh God, I can't even fathom how bad things might get. My mind races through all my options, but I'm left with knowing that I have no control over this situation.

Lord, as I release [child] to the consequences of [his/her] own actions, I pray I would not succumb to the temptation to swoop in and save [him/her] again. It does nothing but delay [his/her] coming to the end of [himself/herself] (Luke 15:16-20). Give me strength to withstand the accusations when [he/she] claims that I "don't care" because I won't bail [him/her] out of whatever predicament [he/she] has landed in this time. I pray You would help me to express my love for [him/her] in a way that does not encourage [him/her] to keep hurting [himself/herself]. May the frustration I feel toward [child's] bad decisions never overpower my desire for [him/her] to be redeemed. If and when [he/she] starts to feel the weight of these chains, remind [him/her] that *Your* yoke is easy and Your burden is light (Matthew 28:30). I pray I would *never* shove [his/her] mistakes back in [his/her] face but would do whatever needs to be done to encourage repentance and reconciliation. I pray You would protect me from any deceptive words [he/she] might use to manipulate my emotions. Whenever I succumb to this growing sense of shame, I pray I would release it back to You, remembering again that I am not responsible for [child's] decisions.

Oh God, be with me as I watch [child] walk straight toward destruction. Be with [child]. Never leave [him/her]. Never forsake [him/her]. Never stop pursuing [him/her]. And give me the strength to never give up on [him/her] either. I pray that this broken relationship with You would gnaw and grate at [him/her] until [he/she] runs into Your arms. You are the God who hears and the God who sees, the only one who has the lifeline that will save [him/her] from the pit.

Like the father in Scripture who runs toward his returning child, I know You have prepared robes of righteousness to replace [his/her] filthy rags when [he/she] comes home from the far country (Luke 15:22). Please open up my child's heart to You, and may [he/she] hear Your voice when You call to [him/her]. Thank You for Your mercies that are new every morning.

MIND, BODY, AND EMOTIONS

Healthy Attitude Toward My Body

Lord, I pray for my body and the way I steward it. Help me remember that my body is not a gift to be done with as I see fit. It is a resource for which I am accountable.

I pray I would not look down on my body for all the things I wish it were, but that I would love and care for it as I love and care for my children. I confess the critical words that have been spoken over my body. Lord, please help me replace those words with ones that elevate this wonderful blessing You have given me to steward.

I pray I would never see the needs of my body as being at war with the needs of my spirit. God, You have made me body, soul, mind, and spirit. I pray I would cultivate this body for my good, and to the glory of the One who gave it to me.

Lord, there are things I can do to take care of my body, but there are also things I cannot change. Please give me a right and healthy attitude in how I interact with my body—treating it with neither scorn nor pride. I pray You would regularly remind me what is within my power to change and what is not. I pray I would not elevate my body above my spirit or my spirit above my body, but would instead treat them both with the harmony in which they were created to exist. I pray that I would not try to force it to do what it cannot do, but that I would lovingly develop it to do more than what I thought possible. I pray that my goal would always be health, not mere aesthetics. As I age, help me to accept the parts that sag, dribble, and pucker. Help me to accept the natural process of aging without fear, resolving to do what I can to keep my functioning at its optimum.

God, thank You for my body. I especially thank You for [part of my body that I am often ungrateful for]. Thank You for how You knit me together, and I thank You that all parts of me that are not working well will be made whole again. But until that day comes, may I never stop giving thanks for what I have.

Honest EVALUATION

Being a good steward of our bodies is itself an act of worship. Ask the Lord if there are any ways you have not been a good steward, either in word or deed, toward your body. Pick one area that the Lord reveals to you and reorient your thinking from merely "I should do this for my health/beauty/etc." and replace it with, "I will do this as an act of worship."

Taming Emotions

Lord, emotions can be helpful. But let's get real. More often than not, they can be like those hypervigilant dogs who bark at the tiniest sound. Like them, sometimes my emotions can be all noise and no information. And yet they drag me along, demanding to be heard and given priority.

God, I pray for my emotions today and for the emotions of those I encounter. I pray I would not feel like a slave to other people's emotions, and that they would not feel like a slave to mine. I pray for the ability to separate feeling from fact, reason from emotion. Not once in Your Word do You command us to *feel* something. We are commanded to *be* and we are commanded to *do*. I pray You would help me take control over what I can control and empower me to react maturely based on what I know, not impulsively based on how I feel in the moment.

I thank You for the ways in which emotions help me when they are properly disciplined by Scripture, reason, and reality. I thank You for how they spur me toward defending the defenseless and speaking out against injustice. God, please show me when my feelings have been taken captive by worldly philosophies or are reflecting things that are not true. May I always have the humility to correct myself and apologize when my passions overtake my ability to reason with godly wisdom.

Honest JOURNALING

Each time your emotions are getting the better of you, ask yourself: *Are these based on Scripture, reason, and reality?* If not, ask the Lord what lies you may be believing, and then ask Him to reveal the truth to you about the situation. Journal through what the Lord reveals to you.

128

When My Brain Needs to Slow the Heck Down

It is so hard for me to be still right now, God. My mind is moving in a thousand different directions at once. You call us to be still and to wait patiently for You, no matter what is going on in the world around us (Psalm 37:7). So please take this meager sacrifice of stillness and use it to refocus me on trusting and delighting in You.

[Take a deep breath between each statement.]

You call us to be still and know that You are God (Psalm 46:10).

I sit here in stillness, Lord, as an act of obedience.

Being still before You is an act of worship.

I choose to focus on You in this moment, Lord.

You are the truth, so I turn my thoughts to You (John 14:6).

Lord, You are good. Release my desire for control.

Lord, You are peace, so I rest in Your presence.

Your presence is beautiful and worth slowing down for.

Lord, You are trustworthy and wise (Romans 11:33).

I will not miss out on anything that matters by being still in Your presence.

You will bring to mind the things I need to remember.

You are sovereign over what is stressing me out right now (Ephesians 4:6).

You have seen everything that is going to happen from beginning to end (Isaiah 46:10).

I can rest in Your provision and sovereignty.

I can rest in Your goodness (Psalm 145:9).

Lord, protect me from the noise.

_____

_____

_____

_____

_____

_____

_____

_____

_____

_____

_____

_____

_____

_____

_____

_____

_____

129

General Healing

Lord, I pray for physical healing over [person] right now. As the creator of our bodies, You know our every muscle, joint, and cell. And so, God, You are the only one who fully knows how [person's] body was created to work. I thank You for doctors and medicine, but we go to You first, Lord, as the Great Physician. Please put Your healing hand on [person and the affected body part] right now. I know You are able and willing, Lord (Luke 5:13). But we also know we live in a fallen world, so we may not see healing this side of eternity. We thank You for inviting us to pester You in prayer, like the widow begging for justice (Luke 18:1-5). So I will not give up! I pray with eager expectation, even while releasing the results to Your sovereign will.

If the treatment is uncomfortable, I pray that [person] would remain committed to [his/her] health and that You would carry [him/her] through this difficult season. Please take away the pain in this moment as we await Your healing, whether natural or supernatural. Please minimize any side effects from the treatment. Help those around [him/her] to give [him/her] grace as [he/she] is unable to operate at full capacity. Above all, Lord, give [person] peace while [his/her] body is hurting. May [he/she] find purpose in this pain that prepares [him/her] for the unique calling you have for [his/her] life. You can use all things toward good for those who love You (Romans 8:28). Even this.

Chronic Conditions

Lord, I pray for protection over my body from the spiritual forces of evil that want to destroy my health or discourage me from my calling. Please block anything that comes from the enemy. But Lord, I also know You use all circumstances to refine us. If You are allowing any of these illnesses because of Your good plan or because You have something for me to learn, then I embrace it. If this condition is a result of the fall, then may I use whatever energy You have given me to glorify You.

Please do not let me become bitter, thinking You have promised me a life free from pain and hardship. I pray against anyone who whispers lies to me, telling me I am sick because my faith isn't strong enough. Lord, I bless those who speak judgmental curses over me. Even when I'm tempted to pray that they would be forced to grapple with natural evil as I have, I know that vengeance is Yours, Lord, not mine. Show me every time where You have used this evil for good, and make it a constant reminder before me that we are to rage against sin, not against the God who died to save us from our sin.

One day, Lord, You will give me a new body. I thank You that I understand this longing for heaven in a way that others might not. Every moment of suffering is an opportunity to desire Your righteous kingdom a little bit more. Give me strength to continue, even when I feel like a drain on those around me. My health is like the widow's coins; the small amount I have to give is precious in Your sight. Remind me of how pleased You are with my every attempt to be faithful despite my failing body.

Honest JOURNALING

Those with chronic conditions can often feel like their bodies have betrayed them. Journal through all the things your body does right, no matter how small (you can swallow, you can breathe, you can sit up on your own, your bladder works pretty well). Find as many as you can, and thank God for each of them.

_____

_____

_____

_____

_____

_____

_____

_____

_____

_____

_____

_____

_____

_____

_____

_____

_____

_____

_____

_____

_____

_____

For Medical Personnel Who Are Treating My Family

Lord, this medical crisis stinks. And it's scary. My mind races to all the worst outcomes. Please put up barriers around the rabbit trails my fear wants me to follow. We are in Your hands, and we know You are sovereign, all-knowing, and the ultimate healer. But we are here on earth, in a hospital, and that can feel far from You.

Please use the doctors, nurses, technicians, and other medical personnel as angels of Your mercy and healing. Help us to listen well and ask the right questions, even if they're also the hard ones. Give us boldness to tell the medical team we gratefully see them as instruments in the hand of God. Please remove any pride or agendas of theirs that might interfere with making the best decisions for my child's case. Where teamwork is needed, give them unity in their decisions. Give them precise insights for accurate diagnoses and courage to explore options. Give them strength and rest in their jobs so they can think and perform at the highest level.

In this chaos, God, please protect our marriage and our family; let us not forget any of our children and their need for care, attention, and comfort. Use this situation to increase our faith in You and our compassion for others. Great Physician, soften us to submit to Your will. We entrust [hurt or sick person] to Your good care.

Honest REMINDER

If you have other children, check in with them. Help them to process what is happening to their sibling. Invite them to pray with you and to ask any questions they might have. Be clear that this is what it looks like to lean on God.

Anxiety-Ridden Child

Lord, please give me the wisdom to be a mother to a child with anxiety. When prayer isn't enough for [him/her], let me carry the burden to You instead. When peace evades my child, give [him/her] the peace that exists only in Your presence. Let Your hope pour from my lips, giving [him/her] reasons to be calm. Let me be tender and compassionate when [his/her] body is reacting outside of [his/her] control. When I don't understand [him/her], stay my tongue and give me the fruit of self-control. Please give me a place of respite where I can secretly cry out to You without [him/her] seeing the additional burdens [his/her] anxiety causes for me. When I can't handle the stress of [his/her] emotional outpourings, give me a healthy release and transform me into a tangible reflection of Your gentleness who can help soothe [his/her] anxious mind.

Help me to set the tone in our home, and carry me, Lord, when my energy doesn't match what is required to face the challenges that [his/her] struggles bring. Sustain me when I run on no sleep night after night because [child] is waking me up as a newborn baby would. Let [child] see me casting my cares upon You so that [he/she] knows [he/she] can do the same. Help me to not make [him/her] feel like a burden, even when my weary heart is tempted to believe [he/she] is.

Do not let this anxiety strangle the joy out of our days and our relationship. Teach me to communicate with [child] in a way that doesn't demean [his/her] worries or make [him/her] feel guilty; give me the words to de-escalate [his/her] emotions when [his/her] brain is holding [him/her] captive. Help me to understand [his/her] limitations yet challenge [him/her] to move past them. I'd ask for You to give me patience, but I suspect that is what You're already doing. This *is* Your training ground. May I start succeeding more often than I fail. Help me to love [child] like You love [him/her]. Fill me with Your grace and wisdom until they become permanent parts of my character, not just temporarily borrowed pieces from Yours. I just can't do this alone, Lord. Help me to feel Your presence as I seek to be a calming presence for my child.

Honest STEPS

If this prayer resonated with you, and if your child's feelings and responses to life are disrupting daily routines and overall well-being, don't be afraid to seek outside input from a pediatrician or child psychologist.

133

Healing from Trauma and Traumatic Memories

Lord, I bring my traumatic experiences to You. Right now, the past is holding me in its grip—and it's like I am still there. It taunts me in my body, my emotions, my thoughts, and my ability to function. Lord, please give me healing and Your freedom in this moment. Lord, keep me safe from the spiraling pain of these memories. If it is better to forget, then let me forget.

The memories come in waves, God. I don't know why they seem so dominant right now. It's disorienting, and I don't know if this is from You or a spiritual attack. If it is from You, I trust Your wisdom and ask You to work in it and reveal purpose. If there's something I need to process, give me a safe, qualified, and godly counselor who can walk me through healing. But if this is just the enemy forcing me to relive some of his prized work, then send him to the feet of Jesus. Be my protector, God. Do not let me be tormented in this way.

Holy Spirit, come and comfort me. I praise You, Jesus, for You are well acquainted with suffering. You went through things that I can't even imagine. And at the same time, I wonder if you are aware of all I have gone through. Where were You? Were you even there? You are *El Roi*, the God who sees (Genesis 16:13). God, show me where You were. Speak life back into me when all I feel is the death left by [the trauma].

Lord, I know I have never been promised a life free of suffering (John 16:33). But honestly, I am still so angry this happened. I'm especially angry at how it still affects me. I don't know how to separate the righteous anger from the unrighteous. I feel like a broken version of who I used to be, or who I could have been. I go back and forth—one minute raging against the circumstances or people who did this to me, and the next, hating myself for not being able to snap out of it and move on. God, give me clarity of thought so I do not take blame for aspects of the trauma in which I was truly a victim. Remind me that it is sometimes okay to not be okay—and right now is one of those times.

Oh Lord, You are near to the brokenhearted and save those who are crushed in spirit (Psalm 34:18). Please comfort me as You promise in Isaiah 61:1-3. Lord, help me to grieve well, not sweeping my pain under a rug, but allowing You to slowly restore the parts of me that were warped by past pain.

I do not want to be afraid of this trauma overcoming me, but I feel surrounded by it right now, God. Open my eyes to see that You are with me—and You with me is greater than what happened to me. Help me cling to Your truth when I am tempted to dwell in the enemy's schemes. I believe, but please also help my unbelief that You could ever infuse such a horrific situation with meaning (Mark 9:24). Lord, as You accomplish Your healing work in my mind and body, may You also be showing me the ways You are going to give me beauty for ashes (Isaiah 61:3). Let me exercise a godly imagination to dream about the ways You could use this trauma to make me an agent of Your love, Your reconciliation, and Your comfort to others (2 Corinthians 1:4).

Be with me as I struggle to understand how to forgive such a heinous event, because I know I'll never forget it. Remove any possible seeds of bitterness that have been planted. They do *not* belong in my garden. God, I know You are not the author of evil, but You allow it in our lives and have a plan to redeem it. As I feel this pain, Holy Spirit, please take what the enemy meant for evil and turn it into the fertile soil of praise. Give me a new perspective; let me see beyond what was happening in the visible world to what You were accomplishing in the invisible. Be with me, my Lord and God. I hate this process, but I trust Your heart. Hold me tightly as these waves of anger and grief beat against my chest. You are the God who calms the storm. I choose to wait upon You, and I trust You will bring healing in Your time. And until then, hold me in Your arms.

If you have not shared your trauma with anyone, we encourage you to find a qualified counselor who is trained in EMDR (eye movement desensitization and reprocessing)— a therapy that helps people's brains to process traumatic memories and release them. But again, make sure you are with someone who is specifically trained in EMDR.

CHURCH, STATE, SCHOOL, AND CULTURE

134

Church Leadership

God, I pray for our church's leadership. Please meet them in deeply personal ways as they seek to guide our fellowship into Your love and truth. Give them a renewed compassion for their flock, especially as they hear and see the worst of situations. Where sin has snuck into the fold, show our leaders how to exercise wise and biblical discipline in a way that leads to repentance and restoration. Protect them against those who would tear them down instead of lifting them up through godly encouragement and gracious correction. Lord, give our church's leaders blessing in their roles, in their marriages, and with their children, and bestow them with favor in our community. Protect the staff from interpersonal conflict or unrighteous division. Protect them from the spiritual attack they receive on behalf of our entire congregation. I pray for an abundance of grace from all of us under their care, knowing they carry a kind of burden for our church that we as parishioners do not.

At the same time, Lord, give me the courage to graciously speak up when issues need to be addressed. Holy Father, we all imperfectly serve You, the perfect God. Give us grace for one another in our respective roles, as we value the different strengths we bring to the table. I pray You would renew our church's leadership when they feel weak, encourage them when they feel criticized, and convict them where they are straying. May those around them see when burnout is looming and step in to offer support. Please show me ways that I can personally uplift and serve my church leaders; help me make their burdens lighter and not heavier. I pray over their hearts and minds as they try to steer our church toward You.

Give them an insatiable hunger for Your Word. I pray that as they study, You would weave together the whole counsel of Scripture. Where our church is straying from Scripture, I pray they would return to the purity of Your Word. I pray for the church leaderships' ability to direct us into Your perfect balance of Spirit and truth.

I pray for unity of mind, common love, and for You to reveal when and if godly division needs to occur. May I always seek reconciliation first. I pray for conviction in the areas where we as a church or individuals have emphasized law over love; show the leadership how to move us toward humility. God, correct us where we have emphasized experiences or feelings over truth; give the leaders wisdom to redirect us without quenching wherever Your Spirit is truly at work. Protect us from counterfeits.

Honest STEP

Ask your church for any of their formal statements (statement of faith, statement on sexuality, statement on prayer, etc.), and study them to make sure they align with the whole counsel of Scripture. Also, encourage your pastors! Make it a point to regularly drop encouraging emails telling them how you appreciate their work.

For Our Churches to Become Healthier

Lord, I pray over our church, its pastors, and its leadership. I know our leaders feel the pressure to be good representatives of Christ, especially with so much damage being done to the culture in Your name. God, we want to be a people who love and invite other sinners into our midst alongside—all of us beggars looking for the bread of life. But God, I am worried that too many churches are sacrificing Your eternal Word for the sake of aligning with the world's definition of love. God, I pray for Your church, Your bride. I pray You would raise up key leaders, watchmen on the wall, who will protect the flock from savage wolves (Isaiah 62:6; Acts 20:29-31). I pray You would increase our church's brotherly affection toward one another, and for honest rebuke to become an extension of that love (Proverbs 27:5). Expose those who seek to water down Your commands and who teach others to do the same (Matthew 5:19).

Show us how to biblically model healthy church discipline: not seeking to shame people into submission but loving the body of Christ enough to uphold righteousness and take rebellion seriously because sin, unchecked, spreads like wildfire through a congregation. Lord, our culture has seen church discipline done in harmful and abusive ways. I pray for Your wisdom on how to purify Your bride without putting loads on people's backs that are too heavy to bear (Matthew 23:4). Protect us from being a church whose love makes people complacent with sin, or whose truth is too harsh to bear. You say the road to You is narrow. Please help us walk this narrow line between love and truth, and have the wisdom to know what approach is most appropriate in each specific situation. I release any feelings of angst where I am taking too much responsibility into my own hands. I thank You for being our good shepherd.

Prayer to Expose Corruption

Lord, I feel like corruption is everywhere: in our politics, in our schools, and even in our churches. The places that were intended to be bastions of safety have turned into institutions of secrecy and exploitation. There are good people in each of these organizations, so I pray Your hand of blessing would follow them as they seek to make wise reforms. Lord, I feel so powerless about it all. But I am not powerless. I pray to the God of justice. And so I pray, for Your name's sake, that You would work quickly in exposing things done in darkness, especially in front of people who have the authority to do something about it.

Where there is corruption in government, I pray the media would have the integrity to report it without partiality. I pray You would uncover the corruption in our churches and give their leadership teams courage to formally disqualify the already-disqualified from leadership so they cannot abuse Your sheep any longer.

Lord, where corruption is in the schools, I pray You would raise up an army of Mama Bears and Papa Bears to not only expose it but also take on the monumental task of running for school board.

Expose the seeds of corruption even within our family, Lord, starting with me. I am not above the corrupting influences of fear, pride, or comfort. Where I have misled our family out of my own selfish motives, I pray You would convict me. If my husband is involved in anything that would tarnish his or this family's reputation, I pray You would give him a way out and that he would take it. Where my children are acting sinfully, bring it to my attention—and if needed, the attention of the other parents in our community. May we be unified as neighbors, each of us looking out for each other's children and holding them accountable. I pray that our kids would not be able to get away with any wrongdoing—that when they sin, they would be caught every stinkin' time.

Lord, I know that sometimes individuals fall into corruption bit by bit and then feel trapped. Where corruption has been accidental, I pray You would privately humble and convict, giving individuals opportunities to make things right. Where the corruption is purposeful and systemic, I pray You would bring to light these deeds done in secret. May we all pray to be privately humbled before having to be publicly humiliated. Oh God of justice, expose corruption wherever it is to be found.

Honest CONVERSATION

Talk with your family about how things that are done in secret are often brought to light (Luke 8:17). Are they involved in anything they would be ashamed of if someone found out? Better to repent and extricate themselves now than to persist and risk exposure by someone else.

137

For Unity and Division

Lord, we are such a divided people, even within the church. You call us to unity, and as long as it depends on us, we are to live at peace with all people (1 Corinthians 1:10; Romans 12:18). But the one time You have not called us to peace is when lies are spoken as truths or evil is called good. Lord, we are living in a society that sees all disagreement as hate. But God, we are to love what You love and to hate what You hate (Psalm 45:7)! What fellowship can light have with darkness (2 Corinthians 6:14)? It cannot. So, Lord, we pray for a godly unity around that which is righteous, and a godly division from anything that wages war against our souls or is raised against the knowledge of You (1 Peter 2:11; 2 Corinthians 10:5). I pray that I would be willing to divide over things that matter, so please give me the wisdom to know what really matters. I pray for the church, that You would sift the wheat from the chaff. I pray that those who love You would be willing to be hated on account of You. But I pray we would be hated for standing up for truth, not for being obnoxious with that truth.

God, show us where we are dividing over convictions, not commands. Show us where we are separating over emphases, not essentials. And God, where we are embracing folly and wickedness, may we repent and be willing to divide for the health of the church. It is so hard to know when our love is supposed to cover a multitude of sins and when compromise is polluting our fellowship (1 Peter 4:8; Revelation 2:20; 1 Corinthians 5:9-13). God, give us wisdom. Increase the unity within our ranks by increasing the knowledge of what You have called us to be as Christians. Lord, make me an instrument of Your peace, but never at the expense of holiness.

(Review the Honest Conversation on the next page.)

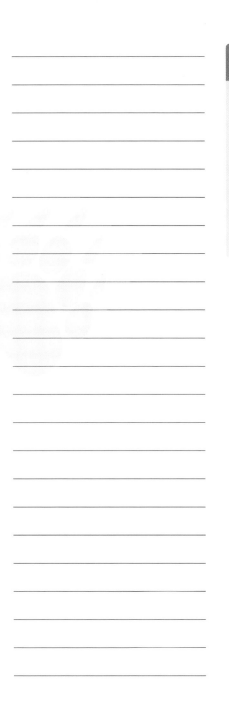

Honest CONVERSATION

God takes unity very seriously (1 Corinthians 1:10; 2 Corinthians 13:11; Philippians 2:2; Ephesians 4:3; Philippians 1:27-29). But He also is serious about holiness (1 Corinthians 5:11-13; 1 John 3:6, 10; Ephesians 4:29-31). Discuss what things we are supposed to unite around and what things we are called to divide from. Distinguish between church tradition and biblical doctrine. How have you seen these two categories confused?

138

For Christian Schools to Not Compromise

Oh Lord, we have seen so much compromise in schools. Even our Christian schools are not immune from the temptation to give in to standards, curricula, expectations, and more that are not based on the authority and standards of Your Word. Oh Lord, help these teachers and administrators to embrace the challenge of staying true to a Christian worldview even when the world calls them bigots for doing so. No matter the pressure that comes their way, may they never compromise or dilute what is good, pure, true, lovely, and best for the students. No matter the power or influence of the donor, parent, organization, or grants who would try to convince them otherwise, may they stand firm knowing that You are *Jehovah-jireh*, the God who provides.

I pray our Christian schools would continue to be bulwarks against the godless influences that are eroding truth in our society, no matter what they fear it will cost them financially. Where and when needed, provide them with fearless legal counsel and wise representation. Guide the schools as they recruit teachers who will train young men and women to fear the Lord while being examples to the world of academic excellence. Give them piercing insights into the curriculum they vet so no surprises would arise once it is adopted. Create an unbreakable partnership between parents and faculty as they work in one accord to raise up the next generation of godly scholars. Let them resolve with utmost conviction to educate this next generation to be ambassadors for You, in the way they think, act, speak, and serve. May each graduating class be prepared to enter society proclaiming the beauty of the Christian worldview through the good works You prepared in advance for them to do (Ephesians 2:10).

(Review the Honest Step on the next page.)

For Biblically Minded Teachers and Administrators in Public School

Lord, we pray for the public schools where Your name is not allowed to be openly proclaimed. Raise up God-fearing administrators into leadership roles. Grant them favor among their peers, students, and the parents. May the fragrance of Christ permeate their demeanor, competence, and knowledge and attract others to You.

Shield both teachers and administrators from the pressures of our postmodern culture that prioritizes feelings over facts and politeness over goodness. Remind teachers that they can teach Your truth without having to cite the Bible, because all truth is Your truth. Deafen their ears when the enemy encourages them to question what You have said in Your Word, and may they be able to artfully incorporate Your truth into each academic discipline in a way that displays common sense. May their teaching refute the idea that students can create their own truth or construct their own reality. And empower administrators to choose curriculum and teachers that promote this truth.

May the staff be faithful employees with stellar reputations so no false accusations raised against them can stand. May their words be true but seasoned with salt and fitting for the moment. Give them patience and gentleness when needed, but firmness and conviction as well. May they never tire of doing the right thing even when it is not popular. Show them when they must disobey man in order to obey God, and provide for them financially if their decisions result in termination. May they have the courage to take that chance, knowing that obeying You will sometimes disqualify them in the secular world. As people of God, please let their classrooms or offices be places where Your presence is felt. Use them as ambassadors for Your kingdom as they steward the gifts and the positions You have given them.

140

Protection for Teachers Who Refuse to Teach Lies

God, we pray for the educators who are being pressured to teach ideologies that contradict reality or deny Your created order. Show them where they do and do not have academic freedom to teach about the Bible and Christianity with regard to history, culture, and values.

Where outright lies are being taught, where reality is called false, or where evil is called good, we plead for Your supernatural intervention. Empower teachers to hold their ground even when pressured to conform. Help them be willing to sacrifice their own reputations (and even their jobs!) for the sake of protecting the hearts and minds of the children they are serving. Bring administrators, peers, families, and their church communities alongside them in support.

Protect these brave teachers from manipulation, deception, and marginalization. May their outspoken refusal to teach lies embolden others to do the same. Lord, raise up common sense in our land, and tear down the strongholds that are choking the truth out of our schools.

Honest RESOURCE

We recommend that teachers (and those close to them) become familiar with how they are allowed to bring Christianity into classroom discussions. The organization Gateways to Better Education is a great place to start.

141

Protection over Freedom of Speech and Religion in Schools

Lord, we are not guaranteed any rights on this side of eternity, but thank You for how You provided for us anyway—inspiring our forefathers to codify the Bill of Rights into our Constitution. What a favored time and location to be a Christian, Lord! We do not take this privilege lightly. These "inalienable rights," however, are coming under attack, and we ask that they now be upheld in our schools. We ask especially for Your protection over freedom of speech and freedom of religion. May no secret or public agenda be allowed to tear these rights down.

We pray specifically that our public schools and universities would respect and honor our right to speak truth and worship You. Protect our students' and faculty's right to express their beliefs on campus even if they are labeled offensive or hateful. Where others would try to unconstitutionally invoke speech codes or zones to prevent them from speaking freely on critical issues, let those restrictions be removed. Regarding student clubs and campus ministries, please protect their rights to freely associate and to set their own standards for membership and leadership. Expose the hypocrisy where double standards prevent Christians from speaking while posing no restrictions on their secular counterparts. We pray that schools would grant equal treatment for all perspectives on campus.

Let our students resist the temptation to trade biblical authority for governmental authority. Help them stand against the pressure to only express thoughts or feelings that align with the secular narrative. Give them the boldness to voice dissent among a crowd cheering for compromise under the banner of tolerance—even if they stand alone in their dissent.

As being a Christian becomes more difficult, train our children to consider the cost of following You. May they count it as a privilege. Let no weapons (like threats or punishment) harass them into silence. As Paul invoked his rights as a Roman citizen, may our children be courageous enough to stand up for the rights afforded them under our Constitution (Acts 22:24-28). We thank You, Lord, that our forefathers had the wisdom to codify our freedom of speech and religion into our governing documents. Let these rights be fairly applied to all.

Honest RESOURCE

People often talk about constitutional rights. Do you and your kids actually know what the Constitution says? Read it together so you can be better informed of your legal rights and how to recognize when they are being infringed upon. We also recommend the resources at Alliance for Defending Freedom. Find them at adflegal.org/resources.

142

When My Child Witnesses Bullying

Lord, I pray against bullying within the schools and on the school buses. I pray that [child] would recognize it in all its forms. When [he/she] witnesses bullying, please give [child] the courage to speak up for the victim, knowing there is often a personal cost involved. I pray [he/she] knows that protecting someone else is always a good reason to speak up.

I pray You would give my child the wisdom to find the proper authorities to manage the situation and that these authorities would uphold their adult responsibilities. As much as it's in [his/her] power, may [child] seek to restore peace among [his/her] peers without excusing the behavior or becoming the dispenser of justice.

Lord, I pray that You would protect [child] when the world redefines bullying to include speaking biblical truth. May [child] be able to model Your love so effectively that when [he/she] speaks biblical wisdom, it is not mistaken for harm. May [child] stand firm in Your Word and in the truth, knowing that truth itself is not a bully.

Honest CONVERSATIONS

Talk with your child about what bullying looks like. Remind him or her that everyone is capable of bullying, and everyone can be a target of bullying. Find out what the school's policy is, and have your child identify which adult they should approach to report what is happening. And teach him or her how to provide concrete information (such as, "Bobby called Jimmy stupid") rather than merely categorical information ("Bobby was mean to Jimmy").

143

When My Child Is Bullied

Lord, I pray for [child] and the way others interact with [him/her] at school. I pray for [his/her] sense of self when other kids pick out [his/her] insecurities and bully [him/her]. I pray for [child's] ability to stand up for [himself/herself] in an appropriate manner and to find a way to remove [himself/herself] from the situation. And if things do come to physical blows, may you give [him/her] the strength to defend [himself/herself] in a way that does not come back to bite [him/her] later. I pray for the bullying to be obvious to those in authority, and for those authorities to take swift action to stop it. May the other kids who witness this behavior also speak up on [child's] behalf.

I pray for [child's] strength to follow Your example, Jesus, loving [his/her] enemies by praying for [the bully] instead of seeking revenge. Where the bully is reacting from hurt, insecurity, or instability, may my child have the eyes to see the root cause and the compassion to speak life. I pray for [child] to be able to see past the bully's taunts and into the bully's heart—a heart that is hurting so badly it needs to cause pain in others. However, where the bullying stems from anger, arrogance, or childish vindictiveness, may you humble [him/her] in a way that silences [his/her] pride. Remove whatever pedestal this bully is standing on that makes [him/her] feel superior to others; provide authorities who will put the bully in [his/her] place without crushing [his/her] spirit. For the sake of everyone who interacts with this child in the future, both as a kid and as an adult, nip this instinct to bully in the bud.

God, give me the wisdom to know how to act. Make it clear when I need to be a Mama Bear, and give me the discernment and peace to address this situation well when I feel like marching in and giving this bully a taste of [his/her] own medicine. May I remember to be the adult in this situation, and help me balance the desire to protect my child with the courage to let [him/her] figure out how to fight [his/her] own battles. There will come a day when I can't protect [child], but right now, God, give me wisdom in how to respond, how to protect, and how to allow You to build [child's] character. There are a thousand and one ways to do this wrong. Lord, be my guide in this situation.

_____

_____

_____

_____

_____

_____

_____

_____

_____

_____

_____

_____

_____

_____

_____

_____

_____

144

When My Child Is the Bully

Lord, please bring to my attention if or when my child is being a bully. I pray for the humility to recognize that my child is not incapable of bullying, for the resolve to believe others when evidence of [child's] bullying is clear, and for the courage to then take appropriate disciplinary measures.

God, give me insight as I seek to discern the root cause. Reveal to me if my child is compensating for feelings of powerlessness in another situation, and help me advocate for [him/her] so that [he/she] doesn't need to compensate by bullying [his/her] peers. If my child's self-esteem has risen dangerously high, may I help [him/her] see [himself/herself] accurately. I pray You would reveal [child's] weaknesses and insecurities to [him/her] and then use that knowledge to cultivate compassion for others. I pray that I would teach [him/her] to use [his/her] strength, beauty, popularity, or any other gifts for protecting those around [him/her], not for being top dog.

Lord, where the bullying was accidental, I pray You would show [child] how to use [his/her] words more carefully and how to be aware of when [his/her] actions are causing another child to feel unsafe or insecure. Lord, I pray You would remove [child's] pride without removing [his/her] spunk. May this be a phase that [he/she] grows out of, and one we can use to shape [his/her] character for the future. Where our family is guilty of modeling this behavior in our home, help us grow in gentleness so we can once again show [child] how to be strong and funny without being hurtful.

I pray that we as parents of the bully and the bullied would be a unified front. May we not be dragged into the drama of our kids. Let us see ourselves as being on the same team to eradicate this behavior no matter whose child is responsible. Thank You, Lord, for bringing this behavior to light so we can work to stop this cycle before [child] becomes an adult.

145

Atmosphere in the Traditional Classroom

Lord, I pray for the atmosphere in my child's classroom. I pray for [teacher's] passion for the academic content, that [teacher] would be so excited about these topics that the students can't help but get excited as well. I pray for them to experience a genuine enjoyment of learning, and for You to protect the class from the students with an "I couldn't care less" attitude that ruin the learning environment for everyone. I pray against any behavioral problems; when the students enter the classroom, please fill them with an overwhelming sense of calm. I pray for [teacher's] ability to redirect problem behavior and to manage the classroom so one child's behavior doesn't dictate the tone for the rest. I pray against anyone—student or adult—who would put the other students in danger; please, God, thwart any plans for harm and keep the classroom a safe place.

May Your peace be present among all students; allow them to leave any problems happening in their homes outside the doors so they can focus on becoming well-rounded, intelligent, knowledgeable, truthful, and kind human beings. I pray You would protect the class from rivalries and cliques; instead, allow the students to enjoy each other, appreciating one another's gifts, talents, and quirks. I pray the class would have a team atmosphere with each student cheering on their peers, engaging in healthy competition without vying for dominance. Thank You for being the God who created math, science, language, and art. Restore my student's and their classmates' childlike wonder as they learn about Your world.

(Review the Honest Step on the next page.)

_____

_____

_____

_____

_____

_____

_____

_____

_____

_____

_____

_____

_____

_____

_____

_____

_____

_____

_____

_____

_____

_____

Honest STEP

If there is a problem in your child's classroom, make a prayer board filled with specific things (or people) that need to change for the good of the whole class. Put it up in your children's bathroom, and have them pray over it every time they brush their teeth.

146

Atmosphere While Homeschooling

Lord, You have called us to homeschool, but some days it is so hard. Please remind me that this journey belongs to You. Help me dedicate my time and effort to Your glory, for Your purposes, and to lay down my agenda for each day. Give me a heart to disciple my children as we walk through all facets of their education.

For me as their teacher, I pray that I will earn and keep their respect—that just because I am their mom, they will not neglect to form habits of diligence and excellence. Help me speak only what edifies and encourages, disciplining from love, not from anger or frustration. When preparation and teaching get tough, help me to demonstrate a healthy balance of working hard and resting well.

Please help me foster teachable spirits that desire to learn. Help my children cultivate focus by not giving in to distraction. When tensions get high, protect them from jealous or quarrelsome attitudes toward one another. Grant me the ability to love and nurture my children, recognizing their unique needs, skills, and weaknesses. Create in them a desire to glorify You in their schoolwork and lives.

Let us never make learning differences an excuse for not trying our best. When we deal with those differences and their inherent struggles, may we not see them as obstacles but as springboards for overcoming challenges and improving character.

I pray, Lord, that my children will look back on homeschooling with fondness, remembering it as a time of family bonding and excellent academic preparation for life. Father, make our classroom a place that shines the light of the gospel and trains our children to go out into the world equipped with Your wisdom, prepared to stand tall in the darkness.

Child's Ability to Learn/ Learning Disabilities

Lord, I pray for [child] and [his/her] time at school. Lord, [area of struggle] is so difficult for [him/her]. My child did not choose this hardship. But You have chosen me to be [his/her] mom. I accept it and I accept [him/her]. Help me walk in the purpose You have for us in this situation. Where I feel guilt, please release me so I am not weighed down. If I have done anything to make this situation worse, show me and give me a repentant heart so we can better move forward.

I pray You would reach into [child's] mind where things are not connecting and give [him/her] the ability to absorb what is being taught. Where there is stubbornness, please show me exactly how hard to push, knowing You push me to do difficult things without pushing so hard that I break. Help us learn to balance acceptance and striving. To never give in or give up. This will not be the last difficult thing [child] experiences in life, Lord, so I ask that this be a learning opportunity in persistence.

If needed, please provide us with a correct diagnosis and treatment. Give us doctors and counselors who see my child as a living soul and not a label. When necessary, give us thick skin, a soft heart, and a sound mind. I pray that You would guide [his/her] teachers' words, that they would praise [his/her] sincere efforts and would not compare [him/her] to the other kids.

God, I pray You would give [him/her] one victory today in [area of difficulty]. Help [him/her] continue to experience enough progress that [he/she] knows [he/she] is able and capable to overcome whatever challenge this learning difference throws at [him/her]. Lord, I pray You would remove from [him/her] the burden to reach a certain level, but at the same time, help [him/her] take responsibility for what [he/she] *is* capable of.

Lord, give us a support group that has already walked this road so they can help us navigate and provide hope for the journey. Thank You for how You've created us all to think differently, because sharing our unique perspectives allows each of us to see what we would be blind to on our own. Remind [child] that what feels like a challenge right now will one day be used to make [him/her] excellent at what You've called [him/her] to do.

Honest IDEA

Keep an "I did it!" journal for whenever your child hits a milestone or conquers an academic task he or she didn't think was possible. Whenever he or she feels discouraged or starts generalizing ("I never get anything right!"), bring out your "I did it!" notebook and remind him or her of all his or her past successes.

Creating a Legacy of Prayer

Julie Loos

By the time this book is published, I will have become a grandmother for the first time. I had a praying grandmother whose example and influence, coupled with God's call on my life, have made me the praying mom I am today. It's her legacy of prayer I hope to leave my sons, daughters-in-law, and now my grandchildren.

The seed for prayer that my grandmother planted in my life took root in college and continued to develop when I was single and newly married. But it really blossomed when my oldest entered first grade. Interestingly, the year I started this legacy of prayer for my children is the same year my grandmother passed away. It was as if God took the baton from my grandmother's hand and placed it in mine.

Long ago I established a habit of prayer for my boys, and we are now on the far side of many of those answered prayers. (I talk about the *far side* here: momsinprayer.org/on-the-far-side-of-answered-prayer.) This is one of the reasons I wanted to introduce Mama Bears to the practice of praying strategically and scripturally. The four steps of prayer that the Mama Bear "PAWS for Prayer" are based on (which I wrote in the first two books) come from the format I learned in Moms in Prayer (MIP) (see momsinprayer.org/resources/prayer-tools/four-steps-of-prayer).

So, as a mom who is a little farther down the road than you may be right now, I would love to share with you lessons and blessings from praying for my kids. May you, too, leave a legacy of prayer.

BE PRAYERFUL

Start a discipline of prayer—both individually and shoulder to shoulder with other moms. You've already started that legacy by getting and using this book. Find a time, a place, and a method that works for you. After being in various roles of MIP leadership, and after training hundreds of women in prayer, I have heard numerous stories of how blessed they have been to use the four steps. Is it the only way to pray? No. However, when I worked on the first two Mama Bear books and wrote prayers using that format, I hoped to help moms bring discipline and strategy to their prayers. And the wisdom our readers gained through spotting cultural lies, the "chew and spit method," and discernment helped them pray more astute, strategic prayers about the worldviews in their culture and behind their children's education.

BE PATIENT

As you develop your prayer discipline, be patient with yourself and with others. Just because it's hard to find time between the feedings and fistfights, don't use your busyness as an excuse. As you struggle to *find* time, *make* time. You are modeling to your kids that this is important. You will be able to speak truth to experience when they complain to you as a teen, a young adult, a new parent that they "don't have time for prayer." You can challenge them to live up to being a product of your struggle. Even if you must ask God to wake you up in the middle of the night or extra early in the morning, and even if you have a bazillion things to do, please develop a discipline of intentional prayer. Squeeze it in the way you squeezed your postpregnancy belly into a pair of Spanx.

Yes, we all need "arrow prayers"—prayers we need to shoot to heaven on the fly. But honing that arrow and drawing the bow back nice and slow with focused, scriptural, specific prayer is how you come to hit the mark of knowing your Father better. And that, in part, will change your prayer life into what Jennifer Kennedy Dean called "*a praying life*—a life of ongoing and continual interaction with God."

As you develop your discipline of prayer, try to incorporate the following types of prayer. *Praise* helps you learn more about God through

His attributes and characteristics. It also lifts your eyes above your circumstances to the one sovereign over them. Be willing to confront your own sin through *confession* and receive the sweet release of forgiveness, and move forward with the now unclogged lines of communication. Give *thanks* so you develop a grateful heart for the intricate ways God is working. You will be encouraged that even when you are not seeing answers, they will come. And then, when you *intercede*, standing in the gap for your children and their needs, you can call on God intimately, deeply, according to His nature and His Word. Leave your requests in His able hands. Intentional, focused prayer is where you are changed as your desires are molded to match His will. And for goodness' sake, if for no other reason, do it for your own sanity as a mother! If you miss a day or two (or ten), don't berate yourself. Just begin again and again.

Be patient in finding another mom or moms to pray with. Corporate prayer with other moms is such a blessing. Having moms pray for your child, for things you didn't even know to voice, is like a kiss from heaven. All those years ago, it took me a year to find another mom to pray with, and even more time to finagle the logistics of praying with preschoolers running around. But it was worth it.

BE PURPOSEFUL

This spiritual prayer battle for our children will be won in conjunction with what is done in the natural. As a Mama Bear, you work in the natural realm, training yourself and your children in apologetics. The tandem effort here is prayer *and* apologetics, engaging the enemy on all fronts: in the spiritual realm as we pray and on earth as we train our children to identify worldviews that conflict with biblical truth.

In Matthew 22:37, we are instructed to love God with our minds, which includes our intellect. In Proverbs 19:2, we are warned that it is "dangerous to have zeal without knowledge" (NET). We Mama Bears are zealous to pray for our kids. I believe we can love God with our minds as we pray using our intellect. When we bring a firm grasp of Scripture to an accurate understanding of the cultural issues our kids are facing, we can ask God for the wisdom to apply to our prayers. We will no longer struggle and babble our Mama Bears prayers. We will strategically #roarlikeamother as we pray.

In compiling this book of prayers for Mama Bears, we have been purposeful in sourcing moms' prayers that come straight from real-life experiences and earnest desperations. We have tried to put in your hands prayers that will touch your heart and engage your mind, especially when you don't have the words to express yourself.

BE PREPARED

As a Mama Bear (or Grandma Bear), your study of apologetics can make you a better prayer warrior. Learning about differing worldviews and arguments against God and Christianity will inform your prayers. Apologetics helped me pray preemptive prayers as well as present-day prayers. It opened my eyes more to the spiritual battles behind earthly issues. When you read the Mama Bear books, you will hone your sense of discernment, and you will be more in tune to things to pray for and pray against.

Use your Scripture reading as a tutorial for prayer. Highlight Scripture you want to pray over your child's life, especially as it applies to truth and deception. Identify ways to praise God through the names, attributes, and character traits you learn. Identify the sins revealed in thought, word, deed, and attitude, both of commission and omission. Confess and ask for forgiveness. Be prepared to watch for answers to your prayers. Ask God to give you spiritual eyes and ears so you never miss something for which you need to give Him thanks. Name or journal those thanksgivings so you have a record of God's goodness and faithfulness. Then identify issues you need to pray about for yourself and others. One does not engage the enemy unprepared.

BE PERSEVERING

In dry seasons, you won't feel like praying. Pray anyway. Amid seasons of smooth sailing, you will not feel the "need" to pray. Pray anyway. Frustrating seasons will make you feel like you are praying for the same thing over and over. And over. Be steadfast. Even when there appears to be no answers to prayer—persevere. Even if you must pray out of a sense of duty, do it! Soon it will turn to delight as you concentrate on the character of God more than the charity of God.

BE PERCEPTIVE

Observe. Read. Listen. When volunteering in the classroom. When overhearing moms talking at the bus stop. When attending school board and PTO meetings. During playdates. Watch the news. Listen to how your child talks about classmates and teachers. Ask God for insight into your child's personality, his or her bent, and his or her struggles. Develop your spiritual antenna to be as attuned to your child as possible.

BE A MOM WHO HAS LONG-TERM PERSPECTIVE AND PRAYS FOR HER POSTERITY

I have no idea how many answered prayers I am walking in the blessing of today that were prayed for me years ago. I have no idea how many prayers I've prayed, over the years, that might not be answered until long after I've left this earth. Even if we don't see all the answers during our lifetimes, am I (and are you) still willing to pray? Do we have an eternal perspective? Do *you* believe that what you are doing matters for the kingdom? For your child's good and for God's glory?

In John 17, we see that Jesus prayed for us before we were even on this earth. We can pray for the here. For the now. And for the eternal.

I am so thankful for the prayer legacy of my grandmother. I am blessed to carry the mantle of prayer. No matter your stage of motherhood, we all have a baton to pass. Will you start your own prayer legacy today?

Pray with Me

Lord, I thank You that we, Your children, are surrounded by such a great cloud of witnesses. That hall of faith listed in Hebrews 11 speaks to what Your people have accomplished by faith. For those of us with a godly legacy, we thank You for family members who came before us and walked obediently, prayed faithfully, and laid down footsteps for us to follow. May we take the baton they have passed and run with endurance until the time comes for us to pass it on. May those who come behind us find us faithful and become the spiritual marathon runners of the future. For those of us who don't have that legacy, empower us to be the pioneers in our families, creating legacies of faithfulness from now to eternity. We know and we proclaim what Your Word says: "Let us run with perseverance the race marked out for us, fixing our eyes on Jesus, the pioneer and perfecter of faith" (Hebrews 12:1-2). We ask You, Lord, to help us leave a legacy of faith supported by prayer. May it be for our descendants' good and for Your glory.

Honest Questions About Prayer

WILL GOD EVER LET ME DOWN?

This is a question that I (Hillary) have struggled with since high school. The idea that God will "never let you down" has permeated the pseudoscriptural "promises of God" and prosperity gospel culture for far too long. But this question misses the mark on several points.

First, what does it mean to us for God to "let us down"? Do we think it means He will always give us what we want? What we think we need? How we answer this question depends entirely on *our expectations of God,* not on who God has revealed Himself to be. And if there is one thing I've discovered, it's that God is the great *I Am*; He's not the great whoever-we-want-Him-to-be.

There are many ways it can sometimes *feel* like God has let us down if we have unbiblical expectations: we don't get the healing we ask for, or the spouse we prayed for, or the raise we worked for. And I would summarize the problems with the "God will never let me down" theology in a single statement: If a theology is not true for the persecuted church, it's not true for us. Period. We are not promised safety, or long life, or a job, or even our kids' salvation. What we *are* promised is that "God works for the good of those who love him, who have been called according to his purpose" (Romans 8:28).

I learned this lesson when I was a camp counselor in college. I had loved summer camp growing up, so I jumped at the chance to relive it from the other side of the bunks. But during my fourth summer as a counselor, I was really, really struggling with depression. I didn't know how to talk to the girls in my cabin because I didn't know if I was going to be any good as a counselor that year.

So I sat them down at the beginning of the week, and I was honest. I told them, "I know what your camp counselor is *supposed* to say. I'm supposed to talk about how God has never let me down and say that He has taken me through every trial unscathed. But I can't say that this year. I am really struggling. You might see me cry. I might look sad. But please know, I am still here for you through it."

And you know what? There was a girl who had been in my cabin for four years with whom I'd never really "connected." She was stunningly beautiful…and stunningly mean. But after my talk in the cabin, she came to me privately, teary-eyed, and explained how she felt like that *all the time.* Holy cow! She wasn't mean because she was arrogant; she was mean because she was miserable.

Far from "letting me down" by not answering my prayers for deliverance from depression, God actually used the depression as a means of working through me! And you know what I did that week? *I thanked God for my depression* and even concluded that if I had to pick between struggling with depression and helping this girl, or not having the depression and not helping her, I'd pick the depression. Why? Because, as a Christian, I value being used by God more than I value being comfortable.

Ever since that lesson, I make a point to take every struggle I experience and try to imagine what the Lord is going to use it for. You can do the same! When you are tempted to believe that God has let you down (or if you are wondering whether He will "come through" in the way you want in the present), it's time to put your imagination to the best possible use. What good could He be planning for this bad situation? What lessons are you learning that will be crucial for the next stage in your life? How might He be preparing you for a future ministry, or to "comfort those in any trouble with the comfort we ourselves receive from God" (2 Corinthians 1:4)?

Now, we don't put our faith in these hypothetical benefits; however, exercising a sanctified imagination can help us develop joy through the suffering and get excited about the ways God might be preparing us (James 1:2-4). This doesn't mean we just smile through the pain. No, friends—it's okay to grieve the brokenness in our world. But, as I said, remember that no matter what has happened, God *will* use it for good if you let Him. That's a promise you can count on!

CAN ANYTHING HINDER MY PRAYERS? (OR: CAN I PRAY THE WRONG WAY?)

That's a loaded question. And I (Julie) guess we should start by asking "What do you mean by that?" If you mean: "Is there a certain format I must use?" then I would answer, "No." If you mean: "Is there a wrong motive, attitude, or purpose with which I can pray?" then I would say, "Yes." The only time hindered prayers are specifically mentioned is in 1 Peter 3:7, where husbands are commanded to live with their wives in understanding so that their prayers will not be hindered. You heard that right, ladies! A husband mistreating his wife hinders his prayers. But before we get all high and mighty, we should ask if that's the only situation. Let's discuss a few hindrances that I have discovered after learning about and teaching on prayer for the last 22 years.

1. *Praying with an unrepentant heart.* It goes without saying that when we pray, we want God to hear us. Unconfessed sin can hinder that communication (Psalm 66:18; Isaiah 59:2). So it's important that we spend some time examining ourselves before we present our requests.

2. *Not praying in Jesus's name.* This is probably one of the most misunderstood parts of prayer. Many people treat this phrase like a magic incantation that we can tack onto the end of a prayer in order to bind God to His promise (John 14:13-14). But that is not what this phrase means. What I have learned from wise prayer leaders throughout the years is that praying in Jesus's name means praying *as Jesus's representative here on earth*—with His authority, according to His nature, for His glory, to build up His kingdom, and with His purposes in mind. We can do our best to pray accordingly, but we can never fully know God's ultimate purposes. This is why James 4:15 recommends we say, "If it is the Lord's will." Know His

character and align yourself with it to the best of your ability. Then let God be God.

3. *Praying in the flesh and not in the Spirit.* This dovetails with praying in the name of Jesus. Are our prayers self-focused or kingdom-focused? Are we praying for our comfort and ease or our character formation? Are we seeking the wisdom and instruction of the Holy Spirit when we pray? It's not about us but about God's will and His glory. The Holy Spirit will help us if we ask (Romans 8:26).

4. *Praying without intention of obedience.* This really got my attention. In reading *Praying God's Heart* by Alvin VanderGriend (one of my favorite authors on prayer), Alvin shows that prayer primes us for action. If we have no intention of acting on what God shows us or calls us to through prayer, why would He answer? We have a dangerous tendency to use prayer as an excuse not to do anything about it. VanderGriend encourages us to be ready to "report for duty" when we pray.

I'm always trying to grow as a prayer warrior, wondering if there is something I can do to make my prayers more effective (James 5:16). That's when I remember that God gives grace to the humble. So, as I humble myself in prayer, He will give me the grace I need. If He knows I am at my core devoted to Him, His Word, His way, and His glory, then I believe He will honor that even when we don't "check all the boxes" in our prayers. But that does not give us an excuse to not grow in our praying life. That is ultimately the right way to pray.

HOW HONEST IS TOO HONEST?

In case you haven't noticed, I (Hillary) am a big fan of honesty. This has worked both to my favor and my detriment in regular life. People know they can come to me for honest feedback. On the flip side of that coin, I sometimes don't guard my words as carefully as I should. (I've learned that not *everyone* appreciates my level of honesty.)

When I'm coming to God in prayer, I find it necessary to let Him know where I am—right here, right now, in all my messiness. The problem can arise, however, when my mind begins to *dwell* on the negative instead of on truth.

Think about it this way: If you are lost and need directions, you have to first figure out where you are. Only then can you navigate to where you want to be. I find that to be the case emotionally. When I feel trapped or lost in grief or anger, I need to identify to the Lord where I am at so He can lovingly direct me out of the pit.

However, it can be easy to stop at the step of identifying our emotions without moving forward. Yes, we have total permission to say *alllll* the things to God—but we must purposely redirect our thoughts to what is *ultimately* true, not what feels true right now. David does this really well in the psalms. He cries, he rants, he rages. And then he starts listing all the beautiful truths about God, such as His faithfulness and kindness. (Psalm 10, 13, 22, and 143 are good examples.) Or David declares what he's going to do in the face of his suffering: "I will always have hope! I will praise you more and more!" (Psalm 71:14).

We can do the same in our honest prayers. Cry out to the Lord, but always circle back to who He is and what He's done. Honest is only too honest when you refuse to move on from your grief, pain, or anger. And if you are having a hard time moving on, then tell that to God too! It's one more thing to be honest about. ("God, I want to move on to Your glory, but I'm having a really hard time. Please redirect my thoughts to what is true.") And then *choose* to speak what is true, even if you don't feel like it. Sometimes your emotions have to catch up, but they will get there eventually with persistent meditation on truth.

WHAT'S MY RESPONSIBILITY AND WHAT'S GOD'S RESPONSIBILITY?

I (Hillary) remember talking with a woman who prayed for the Lord to deliver her from smoking cigarettes. I asked her if she had tried to quit, and she told me she was waiting for God to just take away the addiction so she could give Him all the glory and take none for herself.

While that may sound like spiritual motivation, I wonder how many of us would prefer that God just swoop in and save the day instead of submitting ourselves to the slow process of sanctification? Sanctification does not happen all at once. It's a process. (In her defense, cigarettes were such a stronghold that she couldn't picture ever being able to quit without God's miraculous intervention.)

I asked her how many cigarettes she smoked per day (her answer: two packs) and then asked, "Do you think you could purposefully do one cigarette less per day for two weeks?" She looked almost shocked at the question. Two packs (which is about 40 cigarettes) minus a single cigarette? Yeah. She supposed she could do that. So I asked, "What about for another two weeks, cutting it back to two packs minus *two* cigarettes?" Suddenly the task didn't seem so daunting. She had been so focused on immediate deliverance that she had neglected the ways in which she *did* have control.

I've found myself in similar situations, especially when it comes to my health. There are ways I would love for God to just come in and magically make me a kidney-and-liver-working, non-cancer-producing picture of health. I realized that I have become so focused on the end goal of perfect health that I've neglected the things that are within my control—like keeping up with a healthy diet and exercise. Like my friend in the example above, I have wanted God to do everything with a snap of His fingers when He may be waiting for me to discipline myself in the areas over which I *do* have control. I have known God to miraculously heal in the past, and I've seen Him instantly deliver someone from addiction. But more often than not, I find that God prefers to work through natural means. So I have started praying for Him to change my appetites and to give me a feeling of pleasure when I exercise.

Do not let your idea of where you want to be prevent you from using God's strength to take the next logical step in whatever journey you are on. Obedience may not sound as thrilling as instant deliverance, but it is no less miraculous to witness a child of God painstakingly offering himself or herself up daily as a living sacrifice, doing what does not come naturally (Romans 12:1).

Acknowledgments

Hillary:

I would like to thank Julie for being such an amazing writing partner. Jules, you were with me every step of the way, and I'll always cherish this last year together! We made it through all the tech problems and endless rewrites and reorganizations! There is truly no way this book could have happened without you.

Thank you to Harvest House for suggesting this book, and your flexibility as I navigated so many health issues. I think this book was part of my healing. Thank you for your support and faith. And thank you, Emma and Audrey, for lending different perspectives when we needed it.

Thank you to Ricky Chelette, Katy Faust, Deb Northcutt, and Holly Pivoc for lending your expertise to difficult topics. Thank you to my countless friends who let me call and run things by you—Bethany Woodward, Bethany Franger, Katie Hoksbergen, Amy Davison, Jennifer DeFrates, Alexa Cramer, Sheila Punt, David Walcott, A.E. (you know who you are), my parents (of course!), and the countless people who responded to Facebook crowdsourcing questions. Thank you to Crystal Snieder and Julie Beyer, who made sure I was fed and the house wasn't a total disaster for many a week during crunch time. Thank you to my Mama Bears (Lindsey, Amy, Jennifer, Alexa), who kept the ministry running while I was working on this project. Thank you to my amazing husband, who is 100 percent behind my every endeavor, and who picks up slack around the house when my limited energy is consumed with a project. You never make me feel guilty for my limitations. I can't imagine doing Mama Bear Apologetics without you, my love.

Oh Lord, my God, I praise You that we can come to You in all our ugliness, yet You take our meager offerings of prayer and receive them like a good Father, delighted in even our most unsophisticated attempts. God, I pray that all who read this book would learn to pray honest *and* effective prayers according to Your name and character. Thank You, my Lord, my God, that I don't need to clean myself before coming to You—that's Your job.

Julie:

A huge, heartfelt thank-you to Moms in Prayer International: especially founder Fern Nichols and the women in MIP leadership who have mentored me in prayer for the past two-plus decades as well as the fellow moms in my MIP groups who have carried my boys (now men) to God's throne weekly. I am blessed to have had my sister, Jane, and many friends pray for me during the writing process. I am honored and deeply thankful that Hillary asked me to be a part of this project—you are one of the most talented thinkers and writers I know. Thanks to my patient husband, Todd, for understanding the writing time invested in this book.

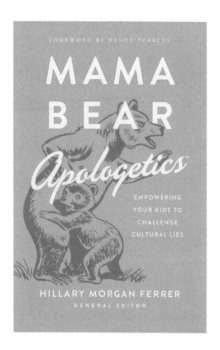

MAMA BEAR APOLOGETICS®

From a group of everyday Christian moms comes *Mama Bear Apologetics*®. This book equips you to teach your kids how to form their beliefs about what is true and what is false. Join bestselling author Hillary Morgan Ferrer in the Mama Bear movement— when you mess with our kids, we will demolish your arguments!

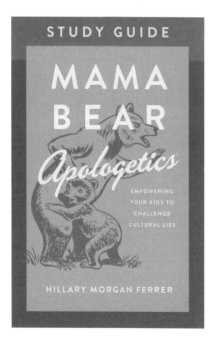

MAMA BEAR APOLOGETICS® STUDY GUIDE

With this user-friendly companion to the bestselling book *Mama Bear Apologetics*®, you'll understand the secular worldviews your children face every day and build the foundation of faith and knowledge you need to equip them to respond to culture's lies.

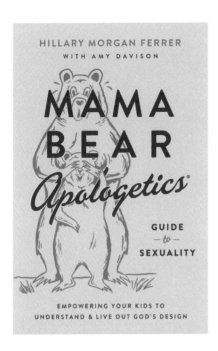

MAMA BEAR APOLOGETICS®
GUIDE TO SEXUALITY

This workbook companion to *Mama Bear Apologetics® Guide to Sexuality* will expand your study of the biblical case against the many myths about gender and sexuality that permeate today's world.

MAMA BEAR APOLOGETICS®
GUIDE TO SEXUALITY
DISCIPLESHIP WORKBOOK

In the footsteps of the bestselling *Mama Bear Apologetics®* comes this invaluable guide to training your kids to know and respect God's design in a world that has rejected it. This book will give you the wisdom to confidently raise your children to understand sex and gender through a biblical lens.

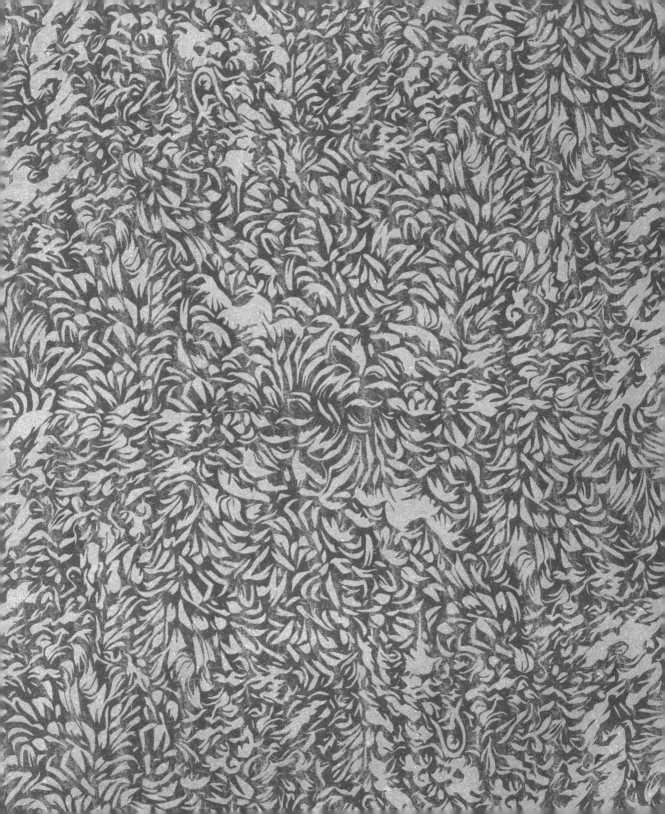